MATCH ANALYSIS
and
Game Preparation

by

Henny Kormelink and Tjeu Seeverens

Library of Congress Cataloging - in - Publication Data

Kormelink, Henny and Seeverens, Tjeu
  Match Analysis and Game Preparation

ISBN No. 1-890946-19-2
Library of Congress Catalog card Number 98-067120
Copyright © March 1999

Reedswain Books are available at special discounts for bulk purchase. For details, contact Reedswain at 1-800-331-5191.

Photography (cover)
EMPICS

Art Direction, Design and Layout
Kimberly N. Bender

Editing and Proofing
Bryan R. Beaver

Printed by
DATA REPRODUCTIONS
Auburn Hills, Michigan

REEDSWAIN BOOKS and VIDEOS
612 Pughtown Road
Spring City, Pennsylvania 19475 USA
1-800-331-5191 • www.reedswain.com

MATCH ANALYSIS
and
Game Preparation

by
Henny Kormelink and Tjeu Seeverens

Published by
REEDSWAIN INC

Table of Contents

INTRODUCTION

In the Netherlands we try to play attractive, attacking soccer in every match, and we play to win. This is not easy. However, the successes of Dutch teams and Dutch clubs (Ajax, Feyenoord, PSV, Heerenveen) owe much to the vision of top Dutch coaches. The Dutch soccer school is internationally renowned and successful because it takes the essentials of the game of soccer as its starting point. Enjoyment, playing to win, maximum possession of the ball, fast circulation of the ball, good positional play and an emphasis on attacking play are among the key aspects.

For a coach the next match is always the most important. It totally dominates your thoughts. And because soccer is so complex, there are all sorts of ways that you can look at it. Coaches must be able to read a match, and then translate their insights into drills that will help their players to function more effectively. This is the most important idea behind this book. In it, coaches will find answers to a number of questions that coaches often ask in connection with game preparation and match analysis. How do you prepare your team for a match? What sort of information can you gain from a match? What influence can you exert as a coach, during and after a match and at half time? What elements make up a good game?

A lot of attention is also devoted to new developments. The computer and video are excellent aids for analyzing a match, and for illustrating post-match discussions with the players. The book also draws on the experience of top coaches in other team sports from whose ideas we can learn a lot in the soccer world.

Although every coach may feel that he spends every week thinking, planning and working towards the next match, there will always be new developments to consider. Soccer is in a permanent state of evolution. In a sense, therefore, it is impossible to prepare your team to play the perfect match, but this does not mean that you should cease trying. I hope that you will find this book a modern, useful aid to preparing your team for the next match.

Henny Kormelink

Match Analysis and Game Preparation

CHAPTER 1

The Match As
Seen Through the Eyes of
Foppe de Haan
Preparation, Analysis and Evaluation

S C Heerenveen is immensely popular throughout the Netherlands. In just a few years it has moved up from the lower professional ranks to establish itself in the top third of the Dutch premier league. Foppe de Haan played a large part in this success story. His achievements have earned him considerable respect.

At the end of the 1996/97 season he was faced with a huge problem. The players who had been so successfully developed by Heerenveen became the targets of big clubs with lots of money to spend. After the Dutch Cup Final defeat by Roda JC, 16 players left. However, thanks to its well organized scouting system, the club was soon able to sign up replacements from the Netherlands as well as other European countries and Africa. In addition, a number of play-

ers from the club's youth team were added to the first-team squad. Nevertheless, Foppe de Haan was faced with the task of building a completely new team. And because Heerenveen had to participate in a European competition during the summer break, he was forced to start early - perhaps too early.

Amazingly the Heerenveen coach succeeded in creating a close-knit team in record time. He himself regards it as a wonder that players of so many different nationalities and languages could gel together in such a short time. This is probably false modesty. The team's good performances were certainly attributable to Foppe de Haan's method of working, as well as the good organization and atmosphere within the club.

In any event the team was successful, and this was what its fans had grown to expect and even demand. They were delighted with the breakthrough of local talent such as Tieme Klompe, but cheered just as wildly when one of the foreign acquisitions scored a goal.

There are plans to market a film about Foppe de Haan's methods in the series "The Dutch Soccer School." In the meantime we decided to ask him for a contribution to this book. Here are his thoughts on match preparation, analysis and assessment.

Match preparation

Match preparation is focused mainly on my own team rather than the opposition. This is why the preparation really starts during the previous game. I dictate notes to my assistant Gert Jan Verbeek while we are on the bench. I use these notes during the post-match discussion, which always takes place on the day after the match. If we play on a Saturday, the players have a running session on the Sunday afternoon, followed by the match analysis. I always do this with the whole group. There was a time when I talked to players individually, but I soon realized that other players were always involved. And before you know it you are talking to one of your players about other players. That is not good. The advantage of a group discussion is that the players hear criticism from each other.

If a player comes to me immediately after a game and begins to complain, I bring this up during the post-match discussion. I tell the player that I appreciate that he was in an emotional state of mind the previous day and wanted to voice his dissatisfaction, but I now expect him to explain his criticisms more analytically to the group. In this way you can prevent cliques from being formed.

At the start of the week I always explain the program for the following days and what our objectives are. I want the players to feel that they also have to accept responsibility. For example, our next game is against De Graafschap. At the start of the week I tell the players that De Graafschap plays with two strikers. The players then know how Heerenveen will respond to this - with two defenders marking the strikers and one player just in front of them. You sketch this without making any reference to who will be playing or not. At the start of the week I also tell the players how intensively we will be training. Before the De Graafschap game, for example, I explained why we would be training less intensively after the exertions of the past week. A game against De Graafschap will be demanding and very physical, and after a hard week it is therefore essential to keep a close eye on the work-to-rest relationship during the preparations for such a game. More time is therefore devoted to other aspects, such as concentration and attention to specific details. I confront the players with these things at the start of a new week.

In a normal week I organize a game of 11 v 11 during the Thursday training session. The second team provides the opposition and adopts the playing system of our next opponents. The players can make mistakes during these games, but it is important that they learn from them. I interrupt the play at critical moments, although not as often as I used to. I restrict myself to 2 or 3 occasions when really important situations arise. In earlier years I tended to interrupt the play more often. Probably I had less confidence in the group, or I wanted to force certain aspects.

During the Friday training session I always deal with the style of play of our opponents, and during the discussions I give the players information about the opposing players. My assistants, Luc Balkestein and Gert Jan Verbeek, have the task of going to watch other teams play. I expect their reports of these games to end with an analysis of strengths and weaknesses, and when I have read the report I usually have a number of questions to put to them. My thoughts, however, are always primarily directed toward my own team, and I only make a minimum of adjustments for our opponents. I think that you have to have confidence in your own style of play. I never turn everything upside down. You have your own guideline. This is a mixture of long-term planning and the lessons from the previous match.

During this training session I always organize a game of attackers against defenders or vice versa, depending on the main aspects of the coming game. Jan de Visser is the type of player who demands that set moves be regularly practiced. How should we play the ball to the strikers? Who should run in at the near post and the far post for crosses? How should we exploit each player's specific talents? Klompe, for example, can pass the ball well down the center of the pitch, whereas I deliberately let Hansma play the ball upfield from the flank. Firm agreements about these matters give the players a secure feeling. They often need this.

A very important principle, which we often practice, is passing to the second or third player and leaving out the first player. The ball is not passed to a midfielder who has taken up position to receive it, but rather directly to a striker.

There is always a match discussion during the Friday morning session. This lasts no more than 15 minutes. I sketch our opponents, repeat what we have practiced during training sessions, and if the players are alert they can already predict the names on the starting roster. This is because I always coach on the basis of the players' positions. The team formation can therefore never be a surprise for the players. I also explain briefly what we will do defensively, and what they can expect in this regard.

On Saturday the program depends on whether we are playing at home or away. If we are playing at home, I usually ask the players to meet at 2 p.m. There is then a light training session of 45 minutes, with special attention being paid to restart plays. Sometimes we concentrate on footwork during such a session - especially if the past week has been very strenuous.

The players had great difficulty in adjusting to training sessions on match days. We did this before our games with Ajax Amsterdam and Feyenoord Rotterdam and it paid off. We also had a light training session before we took the bus to Amsterdam for the away game with Ajax.

When we are playing at home we go to a restaurant after such a training session. That is where I give my pre-match talk. I repeat a few things from the previous talk and devote more attention to how we should play when we have possession. I then deal with our defensive organization in restart situations. After the Cup Final against Roda JC I decided to stop assigning players to mark specific opponents at corners. If the opposing player is more aggressive, or is playing better, then you have a problem. That is why everyone is now responsible for his own zone. You go for the ball and you automatically come up against your opponent. When you assign each

player to a particular zone you have to take account of their heights, and the heights of the opposing players. If, for example, I know that a tall player such as Regillio Vrede of Roda JC attacks the zone by the far post, then I assign Roberto Straal to that zone rather than a smaller player. That is logical. Otherwise each player knows his zone. The advantage is that you are less dependent on what your opponent does. On other occasions I let the players meet just two hours before a game. This

might be the case when, for example, I feel that we are very well prepared and our concentration is good.

The match

I remain relatively relaxed during a match. I have a lot of confidence in the players, the club and myself. Obviously you are always a little tense. During the match, my assistant, Gert Jan Verbeek, monitors the opposing team's basic organization and records this after about 10 minutes. Sometimes you have to make adjustments. I am not afraid to make an early substitution. Against Feyenoord, Vos played on the right flank against Mitrita, who is only 5'4" tall. This was untenable and I moved Mitrita into the middle to mark Sanchez and sent Klompe to play against Vos, because Vos tends to move infield frequently. Last season I substituted two defenders after just 20 minutes against Vitesse Arnhem. Of course, I had two good defenders on the substitutes bench.

During the half-time break I always sketch our basic organization and that of our opponents. Then I issue a few individual instructions. This all has to be done inside five minutes. I usually remain calm, although I am actually an emotional person. I only become angry if I have the feeling that the players are not pulling their weight. I cannot accept this and I give them a massive dressing down. Fortunately this is rarely necessary.

Last season I could make real changes during the break because the players knew my system well, but I am far from being able to do that with so many new players in the team.

Substitutes

Above all, substitutes have to know their place. They will get nowhere by going to journalists and claiming that I will have to give them a place in the starting lineup after they have come off the bench and played well. In fact, that just disposes me to leave them out of the squad for a while. The players have to leave a coach in peace to think these things over quietly. They have to use the training sessions to show the coach that they deserve to be in the team. It is not something to go public about. The same journalists then come to me to ask whether I share the player's opinion. My answer is always "No comment."

A substitute must be cooperative. He should be happy when the team wins, and he must show proper concern for the other players. Similarly, regular players must make substitutes feel that the team accepts them. There is always a reason why someone is assigned to the substitutes bench. He may have less ability than the regular players, or he may have the role of a pinch hitter, or he may not yet be ready for a regular place. I do not spend time continuously explaining this. But I do regularly tell the players what I think of them. And I tell them what they have to work at to become better.

The referee

There was a time when I used to argue with referees. There are occasions even now when I am tempted to do so, but coaches have to realize that referees have a very difficult job.

In general I think that Dutch referees whistle far too often. I was recently in Denmark, where they whistle about once in five minutes, and only then if it is really necessary. In the Netherlands the referees whistle for every challenge in the penalty area. Dutch referees try to avoid taking any risks in that area. Referees' assistants are supposed to have more responsibility, but I have not seen any evidence of this. I also think that showing yellow cards to players who "take a dive" is excessive. It is out of all proportion.

During my talks I never mention the referee, except to warn the players that they should make themselves scarce as soon as they can if the referee is known to be quick to show the yellow card. Sometimes I do not even know who has been assigned to referee a game. That is an indication that it does not interest me. In my opinion you have to teach your players not to continuously complain to the referee. You have to walk away from the referee and accept his decision, because there is no way that he is going to change it. As a coach I sometimes find this difficult, but you have to practice what you preach. You have to be professional. I know that referees award less free-kicks against Ajax than against Heerenveen or any other team, but I enjoyed the same advantage myself when I was at the top with ACV. When you are at the top the referees tend to be on your side, for whatever reason, and the top teams in the Netherlands benefit from this. You have to accept it, and try to get to the top yourself. Players also have to learn when they can best intervene.

The press

At Heerenveen we have a number of rules about how players should handle the press. For example, players can talk about themselves but not about their teammates. Ruud van Nistelrooy did that very well after the Heerenveen-Sparta match. When he was asked what went wrong, he answered, "I should have scored two goals." That is how it should be done.

If, as a coach, you do not want to disclose certain things to the press, you should say so. And if you do want to, you should not try to be too clever. In general, coaches tend to approach these things too complicatedly. A coach often wants to convince a journalist that he, the coach, was right. But the journalist has seen the match himself and has his own opinion. And that is that. Fortunately 14,000 people come to watch Heerenveen's home matches. They all have their own opinion, and it does not have to be the same as mine. I have no problems accepting that. However, the players have to take note of what I think.

Naturally I try to keep the press on my side. I cannot do that by continuously entering into confrontations. I say what I think, often very directly, but honestly and without trying to cover anything up. I think that most journalists appreciate this approach.

Youth development

Youth development at a professional club such as Heerenveen is becoming steadily more professional. You educate youngsters for the job of professional soccer player. As a result some players leave school early and opt for our vocational training. If the players are very talented, that may appear to be a good choice. However, I have my doubts. In my opinion youngsters should choose for both options - school and SC Heerenveen. But the fact that young players choose otherwise obligates you to invest more energy in their education. I think that each team should have two coaches, because that enables you to work selectively with individuals. That is why we employ seven coaches and a full-time talent scout.

Each Monday we discuss all of the matches. On Saturdays I regularly watch the Under 18 and Under 16 youth teams play, and I add my comments to those of their own coach. On Thursdays we always discuss the coming week. What coaching aspects do we want to focus on? What are our coaching objectives and how are we to attain them? Now and again there is a get-together of the whole group. On these occasions we might discuss SC Heerenveen's youth development concept, or how we want to play, or how youngsters should be supervised and supported.

The club has documented its objectives for each age group. Everyone has to draw up a plan based on these, and be able to explain it to the group. I then put forward my comments. The coaching staff holds regular meetings with the club's board. We have brainstorming sessions about all sorts of things. Where do we want the club to go? How can we continually set ourselves more demanding targets? Can we reach position four or five in the league and thus qualify to play in a European competition? We are always trying to identify the next step forward, and how we can best facilitate it. On the basis of our discussions we may try to recruit young players from further afield, or we may extend our accommodation for young players, or we may intensify our scouting activities.

A potential weak point is that we can reach agreements with young players' parents, but they can back out at any time. Mutual trust remains the basis, and the belief that their sons have gone to a good club.

Foreign players

Yes, there are a lot of foreign players at SC Heerenveen, but we also scout carefully for players in the Netherlands. We signed Van Nistelrooy this season, who was the best player in the first division last year, as well as Radomski, who was also among the top players in the same division. We needed a "nuisance" player in the squad, so we signed Samardzic, an awkward, wholehearted player. For the rest we had no choice but to bring in foreign players. Our youngsters were also given a chance. Only one (Tieme Klompe) was able to make the breakthrough, but Ron Pander is also well on the way. The main factor in determining whether a youngster manages to break through is his ability to handle pressure. Younger players tend to put themselves under a lot of pressure. They want to get to the top as soon as possible. If that is your attitude, you always need a little longer. Young players should retain their lack of inhibition, try to enjoy the present, and think about what they can do to improve. If you try to force their development it sometimes has the opposite effect. You find yourself facing a locked door. Klompe is an

intelligent youth - he is studying at university as well as playing soccer. Van Nistelrooy also needs to be careful not to push himself too
hard. He came from nowhere and is suddenly in the limelight. After
just six games he has been selected for the Dutch youth team. A
coach has to be very careful in these situations.

The future

You often read that players will have to master several systems of
play in future. I would formulate this differently. Players must learn
much faster to appreciate what is needed of them in a given match
situation. In my opinion you should be able to switch from three to
two strikers, or even just one. If you are leading by 1-0, for example,
and the opposing team starts to play long balls upfield, you are
forced to play counterattacking soccer. Your players must therefore
know how to do this. Whether you really want to play this type of
game is another matter. But do you know what can really endanger
the future of a club? It is almost impossible for a relatively small, successful club to progress with the same players. Bigger, richer clubs
tend to move in and buy the best players from clubs such as SC
Heerenveen. That is a bigger problem than the discussion about the
number of systems your team needs to master.

In the history of SC Heerenveen, there have never been so many
changes of personnel as this season. A total of 16 players left and 14
newcomers were brought in to replace them. Those who departed
included Sier and Tobiassen (to Ajax Amsterdam), Tomasson (to
Newcastle United, England), Echteld (to AS Cannes, France),
Korneev (to Feyenoord Rotterdam), Roelofsen (to FC Zwolle),
Schoenmakers (to FC Groningen), and Romeo Wouden (to Boavista,
Portugal). Tieme Klompe came up from Heerenveen's junior ranks,
and joined incoming players such as Samardzic (a Serbian), the
Romanians Mitrita, Gusatu and Constantinovici, the Pole Radomski
(from Veendam), El Khattabi (from Sparta), Ebiede (from Nigeria),
Damman (from Beveren, Belgium), Houttuin and Van Nistelrooy
(from FC Den Bosch) and Jensen (from Copenhagen, Denmark).

New project

We are completing a new project, which is unique in the Dutch soccer world. To be able to communicate effectively and quickly with
players, and especially the foreigners in the team, I have put a lot of

effort into video analysis. While others just talk about applying modern techniques to top soccer, Heerenveen translates words into action.

The preparations were started a year ago. During the season Roberto Tolentino, a professional cameraman, regularly filmed Heerenveen's games from a position behind the goal. Tolentino, who also works for the Dutch Field Hockey Association, suggested a new experiment that was first tried out at the match between Heerenveen and Sparta Rotterdam. He used a camera which can focus on the whole pitch to film the game. I then selected the shots I wanted, and computer animation was added. The resulting material was used to illustrate the post-match analysis with the players and we can show the team their weaknesses: "Look, you can see how Ali El Khattabi always moves inside too soon - he is far too nervous. Now Nistelrooy makes a mistake - his concentration has lapsed."

Videotape analysis

Soccer players find it very difficult to visualize the things you say to them. It is much easier if you can illustrate your point with pictures. Communication is essential in soccer, so you have to find a solution for this problem.

It is not enough for me to give a tactical talk during the half-time break. I have to explain myself with the help of a blackboard or a flipchart. I sketch the opposition's style of play, their weaknesses and the way we can exploit these. Everyone can therefore understand me better.

Naturally the same approach is used for match preparation. How can you best explain to the players what you expect of them? This question is at the heart of the new method of analysis through intensive and innovative use of filmed material. Fortunately our chairman is a keen supporter of this method of thorough analysis. He takes a special interest in corners and free kicks. A soccer coach can also learn a lot from the way that set plays are taken in other sports, and the way that one team exploits an advantage over the other. If your chairman is a fervent fan of better analysis, then it is obviously easier to obtain the money that is needed for such a project.

Apart from the material filmed by the club itself every game is videotaped by an independent company, this means that we have a tape of every opponent in the premier division. In the future we will have a video mixer, so that we can edit various sequences together more quickly. During our preparations for the match with Sparta, for example, I made good use of shots from the final phase of the meeting between FC Twente and Sparta. This showed very clearly how the ball is played to Dennis de Nooyer of Sparta, and how the attacking midfielder Van der Laan makes forward runs past de Nooyer. I showed this to my players in detail before the match against Sparta.

It is the details that are important. You do not have to make the players watch everything, or even an uninterrupted ten-minute sequence from a game. You show them selected shots illustrating how a full-back positions himself on the wrong side of the player he is marking, or how he is weaker on the inside.

This approach can also be applied to your own players. For example, Marco Roelofsen used to watch the ball so closely that he often forgot to keep an eye on his direct opponent. After the game against Ajax last season, I showed him a videotaped sequence in which Frank de Boer played the ball to Marc Overmars, who played it first-time to Edgar Davids, at which moment Marco's direct opponent, Jari Litmanen, made a forward run. I was able to convince him that he was standing facing the wrong direction. His feet were pointing towards the ball, and this stance made it impossible for him to react immediately to Litmanen's sprint. He realized that he needed to position his feet differently, so that he could follow not only the ball but also his opponent. The evidence of the film convinced him.

You have to be careful that you do not analyze the game to death. But if you are capable of focusing on the essentials, this is an extremely powerful medium.

Analysis of free kicks can also be very useful and the Heerenveen team has a lot of room for improvement in this aspect of the game. There is a lack of creativity, more and more free kicks are being awarded around the edge of the penalty area as a consequence of the stricter rules and you need specialists such as Koeman and van Gastel, but you also have to think up combination plays. At the moment everything is too predictable.

I remember that Leo van Veen of RKC Waalwijk had a number of fantastic free kicks. His team had an unusual but creative range of options for various situations.

Young players now recognize soccer situations much earlier than they used to, because they are given a better soccer education. We deliberately let our younger players watch the first team to observe, for example, how Talan is brought into the play. You can learn a lot from this, provided these situations are recreated during training sessions. In this way you give players a head start in regard to how they think about the game.

Intensive

Working with videotapes requires intensive preparation and selecting the film material actually takes a great deal of time. In future I want my assistant, Gert Jan Verbeek, to have a direct line to the cameraman. Moreover, he will have a laptop computer when he is on the bench, with which he will be able to indicate which scenes should be selected. This will save time. It will enable the cameraman to be given specific tasks. For example, he might be asked to follow the cooperation between a striker and the midfielders when we have fallen behind and are trying to exert more pressure.

Key shots for the post-match discussion, for example, are the moments when Ali El Khattabi repeatedly moves inside too early and thus blocks the whole attacking line, or where the buildup from the back can be seen and you can see that we play almost every ball to Ebiede. In the first half against Sparta he had 32 ball contacts and, fortunately, in eight out of ten cases he did something good with the ball. But this makes you too vulnerable and predictable. This may be one of the reasons that Van Nistelrooy makes absolutely no contribution to the buildup from the back. He is waiting for the ball to be played to him. At the back, Hansma and Klompe must decide whether to involve Ebiede or to play the ball directly to the striker, Van Nistelrooy. You have to show the players these types of situations and subsequently they have to act on what they have seen.

Another example: The reasons for our mediocre buildup may include the careless passing of our fullbacks and the failure of our strikers to run into good positions. You can only hit long balls for Ali, because he sprints inside too early. Van Nistelrooy is capable of good individual runs but he needs a lot of space. Our left winger (Samardzic) can move inside more, because Jan De Visser likes to go down the wing. The understanding between Ebiede and Van Nistelrooy could be better. These are things that I try to make clear by showing the players videotaped sequences. Animation also enables you to illustrate specific aspects very clearly.

However, you also need to show good points. Because Ebiede moved up quickly, the Sparta players were repeatedly forced to play the ball back to their goalkeeper. And because we have players who are strong in the air, we usually won possession again when Sparta goalkeeper Ronald Jansen kicked the ball upfield.

So you can see that in this technological age video analysis is a very useful coaching tool where players can see clearly their weaknesses and, equally importantly, the things they do well.

CHAPTER 2

Analysis of Your Own Team
by Bert van Lingen

I t is a characteristic of the Dutch soccer school that coaches focus mainly on the qualities of their own team. Analysis of your own team is of great importance. The preseason preparation period is eminently suitable for such analysis, but in fact it should be an ongoing process during the whole season.

During the first weeks a coach observes the available players and slowly but surely forms a picture of his strongest eleven. In most cases the system of play will be geared to the qualities of the squad of players. You might want to play with three strikers, but if you have no genuine wingers in your squad, there is no point in pursuing this option.

When you are sure of your best eleven, remain loyal to it. Coach and analyze on the basis of this team. Even if you lose two games, it is not advisable to break up the team and bring in new players. If you are convinced that you have selected your strongest formation, there is no reason to make panic changes. The season lasts for much longer than 2 matches, and in the long run the strongest formation and the best system will win your team the most points. If this is not enough to win the league or to avoid relegation, then the players are simply not good enough. It is as simple as that.

In practice, of course, many coaches do turn their team upside down if results go against them. But what can a coach then do if the new system or team still fails to win? Ultimately the team's place in the league at the end of the season is what matters. A coach who operates a short-term policy and only looks at the next match will always have problems in the long term. Observe your own team, give the players your trust, and base your actions on your own abilities whenever possible. Try to keep faith with your basic formation for as long as possible, and do not keep changing your team in response to the opposition's perceived strengths.

The Dutch Soccer Association has documented how you should analyze your own team.

The resulting checklist is a useful aid for every coach, and is reproduced below.

Analysis of your own team should, therefore, be an ongoing process throughout the season. Everything that a coach does is crucially influenced by the team's match performance. The team's performance depends on the individual skills of the players, who are combined together in the individual lines, which in turn combine to form the team as a whole.

Before a coach can gain the best possible insight into his team's shortcomings, he must realize that analyzing a team is a complex matter. If you want to do it properly, you have to analyze how your team plays in three phases of the game: when it is in possession, when the opposing team has possession, and when a change of possession occurs. Then you need to analyze the lines that make up the team, the cooperation between the lines, and finally each separate player. The opposing team can also be analyzed, with a view to profiting from its weak points or to neutralizing its strengths. The main thing, however, is to look to your own strengths. Overemphasis on tactical tasks often has a negative influence on the game and its attractiveness.

General Team Analysis
The team's organization (4:3:3, 4:4:2, 5:3:2, etc.)
- What are the players' positions/zones?
- How are the tasks distributed between the players?
- Does the team try to dominate (take the initiative) or wait for the chance to counterattack (passive)?

When the opposing team has possession (defense)
- Does the whole team defend?
- In what part of the pitch does the team defend?

- Does the team operate man-to-man marking or zonal defense?
- Does the team use the offside trap?
- How good is the cooperation between the goalkeeper and his defenders?
- How aggressively does the team defend?

When your team has possession (buildup and attack)
- Does the team take the shortest route towards goal, without much buildup play (long pass)?
- Or does the team circulate the ball?
- In what tempo does the team play?
- How many players take part in the buildup play?
- Are there any playmakers in the team?
- Does the team apply a system of operational spaces?
- Which players score the goals, and how does the team create scoring chances?

Switchover
- Switchover when possession is lost.
- Switchover when possession is won.

Restart plays
- Free kicks around the edge of the penalty area.
- Corners.
- Throw-ins (specialists).

Analysis of a line
After the analysis of the team it is time to analyze each line of the team - the attack, the midfield, and the defense. The basic formation (4:3:3, 4:4:2, etc.) is an important starting point, as is the way the team plays during the three main phases in a match (own team in possession, opposition in possession, change of possession).

Defensive line
1. Opposition in possession
- How are the players marking (man-to-man, zonal, cover)?
- How good is the technical execution?
- Is one player permanently assigned to be the free man, or do the players alternate?

- Where does the free man play (behind or in front of the other defenders, or in line with them)?
- How good is the cooperation between the defenders?
- How good is the cooperation with the goalkeeper?
- Do the defenders try to win the ball?

2. Own team in possession
Buildup/attack
- Do the players run into space?
- How good is the cooperation between the players?
- How good is the cooperation between midfielders and the strikers?
- How good is the technical execution?
- Do the players push up well into midfield?
- How well does the switch of positions function - for example, when a fullback pushes forward?
- How good is the linkup between the lines?
- Who pushes forward from the defensive line into the attacking line?
- How good is his final pass?
- How good is his shooting?

3. Change of possession
- Is fast action taken to avoid conceding a goal?
- Is fast action taken to regain possession of the ball?
- How good is the technical execution?
- How good is the cooperation between the players?
- Is fast action taken after possession has been regained?
- How good is the cooperation between the goalkeeper and the midfielders?
- Where does the action take place?

Midfield line
1. Opposition in possession
- What is the formation?
- How are the players marking (man-to-man, zonal)?
- How good is the technical execution?
- How good is the cooperation between the players?

- How good is the cooperation between the defenders and the strikers?
- Are attempts made to regain the ball?
- Where does defense begin?

2. Own team in possession
Buildup/attack
- Do the players run into space ("off the ball" runs)?
- How good is the cooperation between the players?
- How good is the cooperation between the defenders and the strikers?
- Who makes forward runs?
- Is there a specific playmaker?
- Who pushes up into the attacking line?
- How good is his final pass?
- How good is his shooting?
- Can a set pattern be recognized?

3. Change of possession
- Is fast action taken to avoid conceding a goal?
- Is fast action taken to regain possession of the ball?
- How good is the technical execution?
- How good is the cooperation between the players?
- Is fast action taken after possession has been regained?
- How good is the cooperation with the goalkeeper?
- How good is the cooperation with the midfielders?
- Where does the action take place?

Attacking line
1. Opposition in possession
- Do the strikers try to disrupt the buildup?
- Where do the strikers start to disrupt the buildup?
- How good is the linkup with the rest of the team?

2. Own team in possession
Buildup/attack
- What is the formation?
- Do the players run into space ("off the ball" runs)?
- How good is the cooperation between the players?

- How good is the cooperation with the midfielders?
- Do the strikers play in service of upcoming defenders and midfielders?
- How does the attack function in general?
- How good is the technical execution (challenges, beating a man, shooting)?
- Do the strikers have any special skills?

3. Change of possession
- Do the strikers remain standing for too long after losing possession?
- Is fast action taken after possession has been regained?
- How good is the technical execution?
- How good is the cooperation between the players?
- Is fast action taken after possession has been regained?
- How good is the cooperation with the goalkeeper?
- How good is the cooperation with the midfielders?
- Where does the action take place?

Analysis of a player

Individual players are analyzed in terms of their physical, technical, tactical and mental qualities.

Physical qualities include physical build (short/tall, slight/strongly built), way of moving (supple/stiff), and his speed, endurance and strength.

A player's technical qualities depend on how well he has mastered certain techniques such as dribbling, passing, controlling and cushioning the ball, heading, going past an opponent, shooting, tackling.

Factors such as speed of action, the resistance put up by the opposition, the amount of space available, adaptation to the weather and the state of the pitch, and the ability to overcome fatigue - for example, during the final part of the match - also play a part in assessing a player's qualities.

Tactical qualities are assessed on the basis of four main considerations. What does the player do when he has the ball? How does he react when a teammate has the ball? How well does he anticipate what the opposition will do when it has the ball? Can he switch quickly when there is a change of possession?

When he has the ball, does he time his passes correctly, and can he go past an opponent? How does he follow-up an initial action, and does he have the skills to finish?

When a teammate has the ball, does he run into space to create opportunities for buildup or attacking play (to receive the ball himself, or make space for other players)? Does he go into a tackle properly and at the right moment? Finally, does he take action when there is a change of possession?

The analysis of mental aspects focuses on characteristics shown during play: willpower, aggressiveness, resilience, self-confidence, personality (leadership qualities), and attitude towards teammates, opponents (sportsmanship), referees (discipline) and the coach.

By looking at the players in this way, it should be possible to identify the strongest eleven and to put your trust in them.

Example

Finally an example of how you can translate the results of such a thorough analysis for your players:

- give brief instructions to each player on the basis of his abilities and his positional tasks on the pitch, referring to training sessions/matches (positive approach with regard to the player's self-confidence).

Example

Points to emphasize when in possession (per line, per player)

- Organize quickly.
- Play the ball around calmly, but step up the tempo when the opportunity presents itself.
- Support from midfield.
- Combinations with pass, lay off, ball to the flank, with the aim of putting a player through on his own.
- Buildup play with aim of getting the ball quickly to the strikers.
- Variation and correct choices in attacking play (1 against 1 runs from midfield, etc.), while always maintaining good organization (take over teammate's position; position in relation to teammate with the ball; position in relation to opponent, etc.) through good communication.
- Careful, tidy technique (passing, shooting).
- Take account of opposition's weak and strong points.

Points to emphasize when the opposition has possession

- Adjust organization to opposition's system of play. In other words, how do you play against opponents with 3, 2 (on the wings or in the center) or even 1 striker?
- A 4-man midfield in a diamond formation or a straight line; a free defender who pushes up or a full-back who goes forward; an advanced midfielder, etc.
- When possible, put pressure on the opposition's buildup at the right moments with the help of good communication (directions from midfielders or defenders).
- Analyze the opposition's strong and weak points when in possession as quickly as possible and act accordingly (e.g. assign a close marker to shadow a creative player with good passing ability).

Examples of individual instructions

- **Goalkeeper**: calm buildup, kick the ball quickly upfield to exploit a 1 against 1 situation.
- **Fullback**: In addition to basic tasks, join in attacks more often.
- **Central defender**: Use your body in heading duels.
- Free man: Time your intervention in attacks better (push forward less often).
- **Right midfielder**: React faster when the team loses possession.
- **Central midfielder**: Do not take up too advanced a position in the center of the pitch.
- **Left midfielder**: Try to go past your opponent more often, use your body, cross the ball.
- **Right winger**: Alternate one-twos with changes of direction, try to go past your opponent.
- **Striker**: Make more runs into space.
- **Left winger**: Stay on the wing during the buildup, move into the center when crosses come from the right flank.

Match data

When major international matches are played, an overview of the most important (statistical) match data is provided for the press during half time and immediately after the final whistle. The teams, the team formations, substitutions, goals, yellow and red cards, percentage of possession, number of corners, etc. are all specified.

Naturally this data is also useful for coaches who are analyzing one of the teams from the bleachers. Here is an example of such a report.

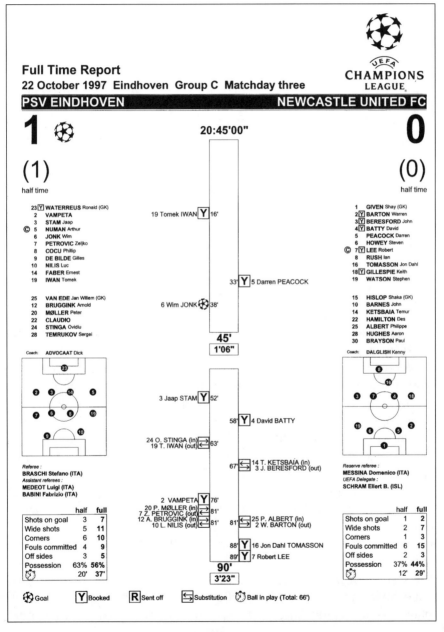

Full Time Report
22 October 1997 Eindhoven Group C Matchday three

CHAMPIONS
LEAGUE

PSV EINDHOVEN   **NEWCASTLE UNITED FC**

1   20:45'00"   **0**

(1)   **(0)**
half time   half time

	PSV			Newcastle	
23 Y	WATERREUS Ronald (GK)		1	GIVEN Shay (GK)	
2	VAMPETA		2 Y	BARTON Warren	
3	STAM Jaap		3 Y	BERESFORD John	
© 5	NUMAN Arthur		4 Y	BATTY David	
6	JONK Wim		5	PEACOCK Darren	
7	PETROVIC Zeljko		6	HOWEY Steven	
8	COCU Phillip		© 7 Y	LEE Robert	
9	DE BILDE Gilles		8	RUSH Ian	
10	NILIS Luc		16	TOMASSON Jon Dahl	
14	FABER Ernest		18 Y	GILLESPIE Keith	
19	IWAN Tomek		19	WATSON Stephen	

25	VAN EDE Jan Willem (GK)	15	HISLOP Shaka (GK)	
12	BRUGGINK Arnold	10	BARNES John	
20	MØLLER Peter	14	KETSBAIA Temur	
22	CLAUDIO	22	HAMILTON Des	
24	STINGA Ovidiu	25	ALBERT Philippe	
28	TEMRUKOV Sergei	28	HUGHES Aaron	
		30	BRAYSON Paul	

Coach: **ADVOCAAT** Dick   Coach: **DALGLISH** Kenny

Match timeline:
- 19 Tomek IWAN Y 16'
- 33' Y 5 Darren PEACOCK
- 6 Wim JONK (Goal) 38'
- **45'**
- **1'06"**
- 3 Jaap STAM Y 52'
- 58' Y 4 David BATTY
- 24 O. STINGA (in) ⇄ 63' 19 T. IWAN (out)
- 67' ⇄ 14 T. KETSBAIA (in) 3 J. BERESFORD (out)
- 2 VAMPETA Y 76'
- 20 P. MØLLER (in) ⇄ 81' 7 Z. PETROVIC (out)
- 12 A. BRUGGINK (in) ⇄ 81' 10 L. NILIS (out)
- 81' ⇄ 25 P. ALBERT (in) 2 W. BARTON (out)
- 88' Y 16 Jon Dahl TOMASSON
- 89' Y 7 Robert LEE
- **90'**
- **3'23"**

Referee :
BRASCHI Stefano (ITA)
Assistant referees :
MEDEOT Luigi (ITA)
BABINI Fabrizio (ITA)

Reserve referee :
MESSINA Domenico (ITA)
UEFA Delegate :
SCHRAM Ellert B. (ISL)

	half	full
Shots on goal	3	7
Wide shots	5	11
Corners	6	10
Fouls committed	4	9
Off sides	3	5
Possession	63%	56%
(clock)	20'	37'

	half	full
Shots on goal	1	2
Wide shots	2	7
Corners	1	3
Fouls committed	6	15
Off sides	2	3
Possession	37%	44%
(clock)	12'	29'

(Goal) Goal   Y Booked   R Sent off   ⇄ Substitution   (clock) Ball in play (Total: 66')

CHAPTER 3

Analysis of the Opposing Team
by Bert van Lingen

The higher the level of play, the greater the importance attached to analyzing the opposing team. Every professional soccer match is watched by a representative of the future opponents of both teams, whose task is to record how they play, what restart play routines they use, etc.

Even in college and youth soccer, many coaches collect such information. Experienced coaches of amateur clubs are often aware of how well the team's opponents play, and what their strengths and weaknesses are. In most cases, information from their players and reports in the local press are also excellent sources.

Another option is to look at the schedules before the season starts. Usually your opponents will play against another team from your league one week before they play your team. You can ask the coach of that team to provide you with a brief summary of your opponents by telephone. The following season you may be able to return the favor by providing him with essential information.

When you analyze the opposition it is as well to take account of a number of general factors. An analysis should ideally be made under comparable conditions. You therefore need to be able to assess the strength of the opponents of the team that you are analyzing. If the coach of a team in the middle of the league standings watches his team's next opponents play against a top club, he knows that they will probably not play as defensively against his own team as against the top club. This is why most coaches in the professional league have their opponents watched several times, especially in away games, because that also makes a difference. For experienced coaches, such analyses merely confirm what they know already, and they are mainly interested in small details that may have changed in the system of play or restart plays.

Because matches between colleges or in youth leagues are often played at the same time, coaches can only rarely watch their next opponents in action. If a coach sends someone else in his place, that person must realize that a match analysis requires thorough preparation and good concentration. Just think of the following points:

- the position from which you analyze the match depends on what you want to analyze;
- you should not try to see everything, because then you will see nothing;
- use the aids that are available (forms, charts, etc.);
- give yourself 10 minutes to "get into the match" and to form a general picture.

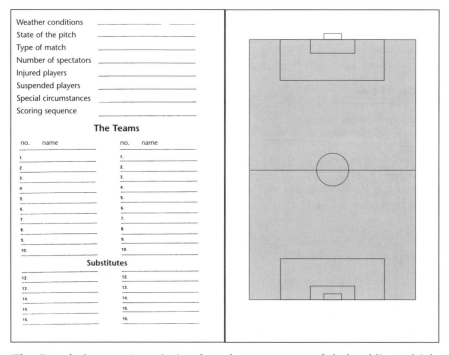

The Dutch Soccer Association has drawn up a useful checklist, which the person carrying out the analysis can usefully take with him. It is reproduced on the following page.

Dutch Soccer Association's Checklist

Obtaining general information

Collect as much information about both teams as possible in advance, such as:

- names, numbers, probable starting line-up with possible substitutes;
- special aspects of the system of play;
- special aspects relating to individual players;
- information gained from earlier matches;
- if possible, learn players and formation by heart.

On the day of the match

- Be on time to record information.
- Note the state of the pitch and the weather.
- Observe the warm-up.
- Have sufficient paper and pitch charts.

During the game

- Pay attention to the basic team formation.
- First follow the game for a while.
- Does the team always revert to its basic formation?
- Are there any changes in the basic formation after the break?
- How does the team play from this basic formation?

1. When in possession

- Buildup/attack
- Which players are involved?

2. When the opposition has possession

- Defense
- In which part of the pitch?

3. When there is a change of possession

4. How is the cooperation between the lines of the team in these three match situations?

5. Restart plays

- How are they executed?

6. How are the goals created?

7. What are the technical, tactical, physical and mental qualities of both teams?

After the game

Put your information on paper as soon as possible after the match.

1. General information

- Type of weather
- State of the pitch
- Sort of match
- Number of spectators
- Special aspects
- Goal scoring sequence
- Basic information and sketches
- Names and numbers

2. General description of

- The first half
- The second half

3. Method of play from the basic formation when in possession

4. Method of play from the basic formation when opposition has possession

5. Execution of restart plays

6. Comments and observations on match tactics

7. Advice with regard to the method of play of your own team

- Advice for following training sessions

KNVB

Do not overestimate

In the context of the whole discussion about the analysis of the next opponent, you should not, as a coach, overestimate the information you have. This will often give only an incomplete picture of the opposing team on the basis of only one match. You need to monitor a team for a longer period of time before you can make an accurate analysis, and even then there are factors over which you have no control. For example, players may be injured or suspended. So use the information you have, but do not let it dominate your thinking.

The analysis of, and attention you pay to, your own team is always more important. Are we ready? How can we use our own strengths to win the game? The answers to these questions are more important than how the opposing team plays.

CHAPTER 4

Match Analysis: An Example

What information about opponents does the coach of the Dutch National Team receive? We provide an insight by publishing as an example Jan Rab's match analysis of the European Championship qualification match between the Czech Republic and Belarus in 1995, which the Czechs won 4-2. Naturally we are concerned less with names than the principles and focal points of such an analysis at the highest level.

The analysis starts with a sketch of the basic team formation and a description of the conditions, which were extremely poor. The pitch was very heavy and partly covered by snow, so it was also slippery. The teams, including the substitutes, the goals scored and the injured and suspended players are also recorded. There is then a comprehensive description of the game in general before and after half time. Each player's name is followed by his number and a symbol that indicates whether he is an attacker (triangle) or a defender (circle). This part of the report is not reproduced here, nor is the section on restart plays, for which this match yielded scarcely any relevant information.

Rab then describes the system of play of the Czech Republic, the opponent he had to analyze, when in possession of the ball and when the opposition had possession. There is then a summary of the strengths and weaknesses of each player in the form of a list with the necessary information against each player. The Belarus players are also given the same treatment.

After the concise information on restart plays, the report ends with a summary of the comments and observations about the match tactics, and Rab's personal advice concerning the system of play of the Dutch team and the training sessions. The whole analysis - text and sketches - covered 5 pages.

System of play of the Czech Republic
Formation 3:5:2 or 3:4:3

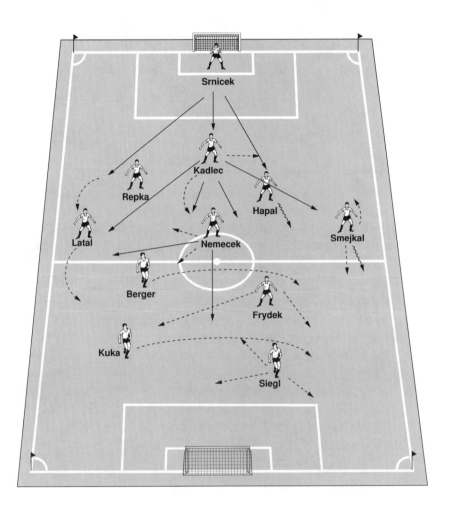

Czech Republic when in Possession

- Buildup from goalkeeper often through Kadlec (also frequent long balls). Kadlec often looked for Nemecek (short buildup).
- Similarly when the flanks were used. The left flank was especially dangerous (Smejkal, Berger, Kuka/Siegl).
- Smejkal was a driving force, building up the play himself or supporting Kuka (who frequently moved out to the left) and Berger (switched regularly with Frydek).
- Free kick was given on that side (Kadlec) resulting in 1-0 (6th minute).
- Berger's goal came from a pass by Kadlec to Frydek, who had run into position and played the ball behind his legs to the advancing third man, Berger, who shot into goal (2-0).
- Berger's basic position was on the right, but he often moved over to the left (left-footer).
- Berger and Frydek were always the players who supported the strikers. Lots of diagonal runs.
- Kuka fast on the ball and always seeking advanced positions (sometimes offside).
- Siegl often crossed with Kuka. Physically strong, always wanting possession. Runs in towards near post when corners are taken.
- Greatest danger is when the Czechs can counterattack.
- In the second half, mainly long balls alternating with fast counterattacks through short, fast, passing moves.

System of play when the Czechs lose possession
Formation 3:5:2 or 5:3:2

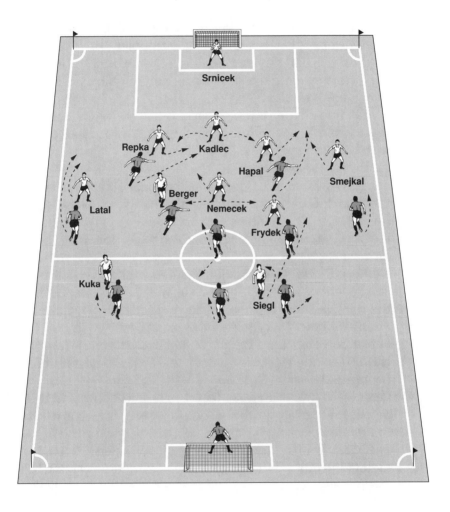

Czech Republic After Loss of Possession

- Czechs retreat to centerline and sometimes further.
- Gave Belarus players a lot of space to build up.
- Kuka and Siegl played covering roles, without shirking hard work when necessary. Siegl is more effective defensively than Kuka.
- Frydak and Berger also fell back, but were often slow to react when the Czechs lost possession. Worked hard, but with only limited defensive qualities.
- Latal and Smejkal covered the flanks. Were not always correctly positioned. Sometimes conceded space behind them in the corners. Switch with change of possession not always good. Kadlec had to intervene on the flanks several times. Latal occasionally beaten for speed by Jusipec.
- Nemecek, who resembles Jan Wouters in that he is always in a covering position, pushed out well to the flank where the ball was, and mainly played on Metlicki (playmaker).
- Physically hard - very hard, if necessary.
- Repka and Hapal are tough, aggressive defenders (markers). They often get in front of their man. Not tall, but strong in the air.
- Kadlec always covered his teammates and controlled the defense, especially in the second half. Not fast, but reads the game well.
- The Czechs often formed a line of defenders 10 to 15 meters in front of the penalty area (sometimes closer to the penalty area). They defended reasonably compactly with 8 players.
- Czechs left a lot of space in midfield, especially when they lost possession.
- Czechs did not use the offside trap (with the exception of free kick, goal).

Comments and observations about the match tactics

- Very strong start by the Czech Republic. Two goals within 18 minutes and several good chances.
- Initiative then partly relinquished to Belarus (Belarus allowed back into the game).
- In the second half, very dangerous counterattacks result in a handful of chances.
- Careless exploitation of situations of numerical superiority.
- Too much space relinquished in midfield.
- Nonchalant in taking chances.
- Too little danger from corners.
- Mediocre organization at free kicks (defensive)

Advice concerning system of play
of own team and training sessions

- Restrict counterattacks to a minimum.
- Mark the strikers closely.
- Restrict long passes to a minimum.
- Do not concede space in the corners.
- Force left flank of Czech team to defend.
- Spread the ball during buildup.
- Play the ball quickly to the midfielders.
- Switch quickly when possession is gained. Use the available space.
- Create 2 against 1 situations on the flanks and make individual runs.
- Follow up on shots at goal, because the goalkeeper sometimes fails to hold the ball.

CHAPTER 5

The Tactical Talk

The tactical talk comes in a variety of forms. One coach may restrict himself to the essentials, while another may put on a one-man show. One coach may involve his players, while another - weaker - coach may regard such a step as a threat to his authority.

Scientific research has shown that the concentration of the players, and therefore their ability to absorb what the coach says, decreases significantly after about ten minutes. Tactical talks should, therefore, not last too long. Moreover, you have lots of opportunities for explaining the tactics for the next game during the coaching sessions before the talk. Coaches often ask what the best time is to hold the talk, and therefore also to announce the lineup. It is difficult to give a clear answer. In the case of regular players, an early announcement can help to ensure a good preparation for the next match, but disappointed players may cause a lot of disquiet. In addition, players may be injured on the day before the match and the team will then have to be adjusted.

A tactical discussion shortly before the match is certainly more practical in the college and youth sphere, but this imposes restrictions on the duration and form of the talk. The players' minds are usually already focused on the match, and it is impossible for players and coaches to engage in genuine discussions about the game plan. You can agree with the group to save your thoughts for the post-match discussion.

The Dutch Soccer Association's view of the tactical talk is given below.

What is the right time for a tactical talk/account
This depends on the purpose.
a. **Well before the match** (in college or youth soccer, for example, immediately after the final training session). One problem is that so much can change before the match starts (with regard to weather, personnel, etc.).

b. Shortly before the match
Often more convenient, but the talk then has to be to the point and should certainly not last longer than 10 to 15 minutes.

c. After the match
For example, at the first subsequent training session. The talk/account must then be seen as a sort of assessment and can serve as a way of reaching agreement about the following training sessions.

d. Individual talks and talks with the lines of the team
These can be held at any time. Especially in midweek, between training sessions.

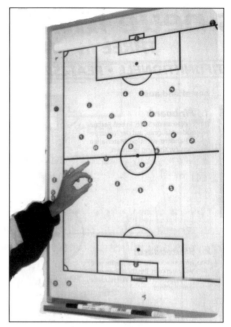

How do I do this?
1. Giving an introduction
Indicate what you want to talk about.
a. Your own team.
b. The opposition.
Announce the lineup.

2. Deciding on the content
a. Provide information about the opposing team, the strengths and weaknesses of individuals and lines, and any special aspects of restart plays.
b. Provide information about your own lineup. Explain the formation and impart any other important information.
c. Provide information about specific circumstances such as:
   • the nature of the match (for example, a league or cup game);
   • the pitch;
   • the weather;
   • importance of the match in view of the team's league position.

d. Explain the system of play - defense/buildup/attack.
e. Give brief summaries.

3. Work methodically
Above all proceed methodically, and do not jump randomly from one topic to another. This applies especially to your treatment of defense, buildup and attack. Work this through systematically.

4. Practical approach
Try to work as selectively as possible. Treat the information succinctly. Ensure that what you say is comprehensible and can be translated into practice. A good yardstick is often the players' reactions to what you say. Make regular use of practical examples.

5. Delivery
Try to impart enthusiasm through gesture, posture and tone. Keep the players alert and attentive, and insist on total concentration.

6. Contact with the players
It is certainly not forbidden, and is even desirable, to sometimes ask one or more players for their opinions on, or solutions to, a tactical problem. Consider players' questions thoroughly and answer them with conviction.

7. Execution
After imparting the general information, such as the team lineup, go quickly to the heart of the talk. Some general aspect should serve as a springboard for treating core aspects in relation to the team, the lines of the team and the individual players. Try to avoid making this a match report. Make sure the players always know your intentions. Use the board to emphasize or illustrate an important point. Tell the squad what conclusions you have drawn, because these are of primary importance. Naturally these conclusions must be paired with explanations of tactical solutions and their correct implementation on the pitch.

Encourage suggestions, questions and comments from the squad. A humorous remark can sometimes help. Be yourself, be calm and thoughtful, and give concrete answers to concrete questions whenever possible.

Tactical Board

Think hard about how you will sketch the basic formation on the board. The positions of the players' names can indicate the principles of a tactical plan. If you want to keep the play as far away as possible from your own goal, write the players' names in the opposing team's half. If you anticipate an even struggle, write the names in the zone around the centerline. If the opposing team is much stronger than yours, write the names in your own half.

If the players are familiar with this approach, you can impart a lot of information in a very short time at the start of the talk.

CHAPTER 6

The Match As Seen Through he Eyes of the Chief Observer for the Dutch National Team: Jan Rab

*T**he** Dutch Soccer Association's course for top players has attracted a lot of media attention. Players such as Ronald Koeman, Johan Neeskens, Frank Rijkaard and Ruud Gullit clearly have the ambition to succeed as coaches (as evidenced by Rijkaard's appointment as National Team Coach following the '98 World Cup). On the basis of their considerable experience, the service they have rendered as players and their participation at the highest level in World Cups, European Championships and European Cups, they can obtain the Netherlands' highest coaching qualification by taking a specially designed course. The players benefit especially from the fact that the course dates are set with an eye to the wishes and work of the (former) stars. The Dutch Soccer Association firmly insists that the demands made on the players hardly differ from those made on the coaches who are currently following the regular course to become professional soccer coaches.*

40

As a lecturer, Jan Rab is closely involved with the course for top players. The players profit from the experience he has gained during his many years as an observer, as a coach and as the man who makes the match analyses during major tournaments in which the Netherlands is playing.

The match is naturally at the heart of the course. The match is the starting point for analyses, discussions and training sessions. Rab is one of the counselors during this learning process. He knows how top players look at a match.

Jan Rab: This course again shows that everyone looks at a match differently. This has to do with your experience as a player and a coach, and your soccer philosophy. It also depends on the position where you played in the team. Top players' backgrounds also play an important role. Gullit looks at the game differently to Neeskens, and Rijkaard does not look at it the same way as Koeman or Krol. The position they played is often crucial to their ideas about the game. Defenders analyze the game from a defender's point of view. But if you talk to Ruud Gullit about the match between Chelsea and Arsenal, you realize that his analysis is based on aspects of the buildup and attack. And Cruyff undoubtedly views the game in a different light to Ronald Spelbos.

The analyses that the players submit after watching a match together also reflect this. For example, we took a number of the course participants to watch the match between Feyenoord and De Graafschap. Feyenoord's main defensive problem was that the four-man defensive line had no answer to De Graafschap's pattern of play with one advanced striker backed up by two central strikers behind him (like the top of a pyramid). The Feyenoord players were unsure how to mark the opposing strikers, especially in view of the fact that one of the Feyenoord defenders, Picun, always had to remain as the free man in the defense. This was why Feyenoord's coach, Arie Haan, soon ordered Boateng and Van Gobbel to switch positions in the first half. This sort of crucial aspect is soon noticed by the course participants.

Advantage

There is an advantage that you have as a former top player. On the other hand, it is no guarantee that you will become a top coach.

The man in the street thinks that a top player should always be able to coach a team. But there is all the difference in the world between playing soccer and coaching it.

This is why top players are not simply presented with a coaching diploma. They must invest a lot of time and effort. Koeman and Neeskens, for example, are serving a sort of apprenticeship with the Dutch National Team. It is not just a matter of analyzing a match. How do you organize your training sessions, and what do you emphasize in your team talks?

It is clear that these top players have very definite opinions based on their wide experience, and they know how to communicate these opinions. After Frank Rijkaard had watched FC Utrecht, he was able to describe in detail how he would let the team play if he were the coach. You notice that his ideas are strongly influenced by the time he spent as a player with AC Milan. Rijkaard assumes that there will be a clear division of tasks in a 4:4:2 formation. That one striker will play well forward and the other will play off him. He also prefers a midfield with two offensive wide players and two central controlling players, who always play a supporting role when the wide midfielders have the ball.

He put these ideas into practice in a training session with fixed attacking patterns, which eventually resulted in attackers playing against defenders and a large sided game.

The course participants look at one specific match, but it is important to look beyond a match. To do this you must learn the ins and outs of a team, and watch it playing several times. Ronald Koeman was given the task of observing PSV Eindhoven play against Newcastle United, and to assess how PSV stood in relation to other European top clubs. Can it play a decisive role in the European Champions League? Could this team reach the European top, and what potential problems will it face? This sort of analysis also forms part of the course, and requires the participants to look at a match in a totally different way.

Matches and match analyses are central to the course for aspiring professional soccer coaches.

During the course, each three-day session focuses on one club. This year they looked at SC Heerenveen, Fortuna Sittard and Feyenoord. Four of the course participants have to attend the coaching sessions and matches of the relevant club. During the course sessions, two of the participants hold a post-match talk about a game. One of them delivers an analysis of the match (system of play when in possession and when not) and the restart plays. The other analyzes the strengths and weaknesses of the team and suggests changes to the game plan. A general discussion then takes place, in which the club coach plays a leading role. The two other participants who have watched the club give a training session, in which they take on the roles of the coach and assistant coach of the club. It is a pity when the squad is not complete, as is often the case, but this is a situation that coaches often encounter in their work anyway. Incidentally, top players also find it difficult to give a training session based on shortcomings that they have identified. Like many other top players, Jan Wouters, who is one of the course participants, now realizes that it would have been a good idea to document his experience with various coaches. Wim Janssen did this during his career, and admits that this has been of great benefit to him.

Chief observer for the Dutch National Team

It is interesting to compare how I analyze matches today with when I started coaching 20 years ago. Initially you try to see everything. But as you become more experienced, you learn to look at the essentials of the game. During a match you are more likely to ask yourself questions. In the past I did not do this. For example, during the match between Feyenoord and Willem II, I soon began to wonder why a team such as Feyenoord was playing so defensively. I then asked myself what I would have done as the coach, and how I would change things. Looking for the answers to these questions brings you faster to the heart of the matter. Sometimes this works well, sometimes less well. In particular, if you observe a team several times you try to get inside the mind of the coach. Because I watched a lot of Belgium's games prior to the 1998 World Cup for Guus Hiddink I felt that I knew which substitutions the Belgian coach, George Leekens, would make. You base this on the substitutions he made in the previous games. This is the interesting aspect of my job as an observer.

Sometimes Guus Hiddink simply reads the analyses, and sometimes he has all sorts of specific questions. The Dutch Soccer Association is now setting up a sort of database. For example, we have data about all of the matches played in the COPA America, so that we will not be faced with any surprises during the World Cup. We started the real work after the draw for the World Cup took place in December. We are now able to link the computer and the video-tape images so that we can find the relevant shots more quickly.

Video

The Dutch Soccer Association recognizes that videotape can play a large part in the analysis of opponents and we have been very busy with a lot of developments in this field, which were extremely useful and important to our match preparation during the World Cup. Naturally we have special software to help us to select the relevant images. The idea behind this is to make the process of analysis more uniform.

I have already said that everyone has their own way of looking at a game from the bleachers. A tape of the game is an excellent way of demonstrating what really happened. We, the lecturers, always make a list of items that the course participants should have seen.

We do this on the basis of a checklist which always has the same structure:

- basic formation;
- general characteristics of a match;
- system of play when in possession;
- system of play when not in possession;
- restart plays;
- conclusions.

Having the same structure is no guarantee of uniformity. It is not very difficult to input the existing match form into the computer, but this alone is not enough to ensure a uniform way of looking at a match. It is important that we find a structure for assessing soccer situations. For example, you might watch Feyenoord and note that Van Gobbel was very active in buildup and attacking moves, and pushed forward frequently. Another coach, watching the same game, might feel that Van Gobbel did not achieve much when he went forward.

What are the causes of these differences? You might well be agreed on how many times Van Gobbel pushed forward, but this tells you nothing about the quality of his involvement. Did he time his runs well? Did he achieve anything when he went forward? The Dutch Soccer Association is trying to create a structure that will encompass all of these aspects. We have developed a checklist for this too.

In possession
Team task: Buildup
Ratings
- Excellent: Scoring opportunities are created.
- Positive: Buildup results in an attack.
- Neutral: Positional play sustained during buildup.
- Negative: Possession is lost.

Team task: Attack
Ratings
- Excellent: Goal is scored.
- Positive: Scoring opportunities are created.
- Neutral: Positional play sustained during attack or possession is retained.
- Negative: Possession is lost.

Team task: Scoring
Ratings
- Goal is either scored or not.

Not in possession
Team task: Harass opposition/intercept ball
Ratings
- Excellent: Ball is won/intercepted.
- Positive: Forward pass or run is prevented.
- Neutral: Positional play sustained.
- Negative: No attempt to harass opposition/attempt at screening is outplayed.

Team task: Holding up opposition's progress/chasing/tackling
Ratings
- Excellent: Possession is recovered.
- Positive: Forward pass or run is prevented.
- Neutral: Screening and harassing.
- Negative: No attempt at holding up progress; attempt is out played.

Team task: Preventing opposition from scoring
Ratings
* Goal is either scored or not.

We can now use the checklist to look at a situation in which the buildup starts with the goalkeeper. This makes it clearer why such an analysis is more reliable. An excellent rating is awarded if the goalkeeper is capable of putting a teammate in a scoring position by means of a long kick. An example is Van der Sar's kick during the 1996 European Championship, from which Bergkamp immediately scored.

The positive rating is earned if the goalkeeper enables another player to make an attacking run. The neutral rating means that the goalkeeper enabled his teammates to retain possession. The negative rating is earned if the goalkeeper's kick or throw results in loss of possession.

This assessment method has been used as the basis for developing new software. The coach is able to sit on the bench with a laptop rather than a pen and paper and we were able to use this system during the World Cup in France. With the help of a laptop, we were able to select useful images from a match for the post-match discussion or the match analysis. During the preparation for a game, Guus Hiddink was able to confront the players with relevant video tape from Roberto Tolentino who translated the computer data into video images. Coding allowed him to immediately show shots illustrating soccer problems relating to defending against corners, or to the buildup play of the central midfielder.

Making such compilation tapes used to take up a lot of time. This method is much faster and more efficient. Hans Jorritsma, in particular, worked hard to ensure that this latest form of analysis was operational in France.

Trend

I watch a lot of matches and there have been many developments in modern soccer. I am a supporter of zonal defense and the trend in Europe has also been in this direction recently. The advantage is that, if you operate this system well, you will not encounter many positional and defensive problems. Zonal defense allows you to defend further away from your own goal, and if you gain possession the players can join in the buildup play from their own positions. There are therefore big advantages for your defensive organization. One disadvantage is that, if you do not operate this system well, one pass can outplay a four-man defensive line. If you play a five-man defensive line, like the Germans, your defense is more secure, but this limits your buildup and attacking options. This has been described in detail in the book "Zone Play: A Tactical and Technical Handbook" by Angelo Pereni and Michele Di Cesare.

In midfield, more and more teams are choosing two controlling players in the center. PSV Eindhoven does this with Jonk and Cocu. I prefer a diamond formation. Especially if your attacking midfielder, who is positioned at the tip of the diamond, is a creative player, like Litmanen of Ajax. This gives the team a better shape.

In attack, I think it is a shame that so few teams in the Dutch league play with three strikers. Perhaps this is because I used to be a winger myself. There is not a lot of difference between a winger who plays in a withdrawn position and an attacking midfielder. The important factor is the attacking creativity of the relevant player. I regret seeing a player like Feyenoord's Bronckhorst in the fullback position. This was a consequence of Feyenoord's defensive system under coach Arie Haan, who insists on playing with a free man. You can identify these problems quickly from the bleachers. It is then interesting to try to think of solutions. I do this all the time. Due to my job, I can no longer just sit back and enjoy a match. I always observe it in a critical way, but this applies to most coaches, of course.

CHAPTER 7

The Match as Seen Through the Eyes of the Assistant Coach: Ernie Brandts

*E*rnie Brandts coaches the second team of PSV Eindhoven. He also *coaches the Under 16 team of Unitas twice each week. But this is not all. Match-related work is probably his main field of activity. Coaching the second team, making match analyses for the first team, analyzing potential new players for PSV - Ernie Brandts has a lot to say about the ins and outs of a game.*

Team Selection

Brandts: I always think things over and I am always willing to listen to other people's opinions, but I am the one who decides who will play, otherwise the club should have employed someone else. For instance, I might discuss the line-up with the experienced players.

When I was a player at Roda JC, Rob Baan was the coach. He would sometimes tell me to regulate a situation myself. I was the team captain, and we had to play against PSV, who had Romario and Gillhaus as strikers. I sat down together with EugÉne Hansen and Piet Wilschut and we discussed how we should play. Baan then came in and asked us what we had decided to do. He listened to us and agreed. As a player, this made you think for yourself. And as a coach, I would want to take the same approach as Baan. I would also tell younger players who they are going to play against, and ask them how they think they should approach this. I know that Advocaat does this with players such as Jonk, Valckx and Stam. It would be foolish not to make use of their experience. Ultimately, however, you are the one who decides what will happen. A lot depends on the composition of your squad. One year later it was not possible to work this way any longer at Roda, because a lot of new players were brought in who were less willing to accept responsibility.

I am always prepared to discuss things. Players at PSV sometimes overestimate themselves. I point out their shortcomings. They have to know what they can do, and they have to put everything into the training sessions. Players have to show what they can do by performing on the pitch, not by talking.

You will sometimes choose a certain player because you have faith in him, and during the match you see that he was not yet ready. Sometimes I make a choice even though I am not convinced that it is right. But some choices cannot be logically justified. You might choose purely instinctively. You simply feel that things will improve if you make a certain decision. This is normal - after all, you cannot do everything on the basis of logical reasoning; instinct also has something to do with your know-how. I have no problem with telling a player that he is not playing because my instinct tells me that someone else is the better choice. You have to have faith in your instinct. I certainly do not let myself be influenced by a factor such as how easy or difficult a player is to handle. Some players are always more difficult than others, but that is not reflected in the team sheet. The main consideration is the result. A coach is always judged on results. You have to be honest.

Picking players who are not 100% fit
The decision to play an injured player depends on how important to

the team that player is, and how desperately you need him. In general my players have to be 100 percent fit. If they are only 90 percent fit, then I pick someone else. I do not want to take the risk that they will not be able to continue after only 20 minutes. A player must never keep quiet about an injury. If he does, the team may suffer. Players must accept their responsibility to the team rather than themselves in these matters. This is very important, and is an aspect of discipline.

Reading The Game

When I first came to PSV as a coach, I looked at games differently to now. Initially you watch specific players, then you look at both teams. Now that I have been a coach for a longer period, I look at my own team. What is the team doing well, and what is going wrong? I also look at our opponents. What is their system of play, and are they playing with two or three strikers? That sort of thing. When I am with the second team, I look a lot more at my own team than at the opposition's system of play. If I sit next to Advocaat on the bench, it is my task to make analyses for the first team, and I automatically devote more time to observing the players of the opposing team. Questions such as, "Is this player doing what we expected - is he playing in the way that the analysis described?" In general I start with the opposition's system of play. Then I look at where the buildup starts, and how the ball is played to the strikers, and whether the team plays a long or a short passing game. When possession is lost, where do the opposition players start to challenge our players, do they pressure us, do they push a man forward, do they play a sweeper, do they try to prevent long passes from being made? Each team has its strong and weak points, and you try to identify them.

I once saw a game in Belgium and I could not recognize any system at all. Everything was chaotic. Usually you only need ten minutes to see how the teams play with regard to each other, but in this case it took half an hour. You wonder how it is possible. Such teams simply have no system of play.

If your team has to play against an offensively strong but defensively weak opponent, do you choose to play an attacking game or a defensive one?

You can defend by playing an attacking game and falling back when you lose the ball. Counter-attacking soccer yields the best results. That has been proved. It depends on the players you have available. Last season we tried to win every game. This year we have fewer first team players available. The present squad is doing well, but is far from good enough. You cannot be a perfect soccer player at 19. Everything can be improved - ball control, passing, speed, the coordination between seeing and doing. But the starting point of a match is that you want to win, although you have to recognize realities. A point won against Ajax is a good result, but against other teams only a win is good enough. As the game progresses you decide whether to pressure the opposition or to fall back towards your own goal. You cannot direct this from the sideline. The players have the freedom to adopt either solution. It would be wrong to deprive players of all spontaneity. Let them act creatively - they can only learn from it. If they can they should alternate pressing play with falling back. The disadvantage of pressing is you take away your own space. If you have fast strikers, it is better to fall back and then break out quickly when you win the ball again.

Pre-Game

The players do some running then they do some light stretching exercises - diagonal steps, lifting their knees, etc. Then they pair off, each pair with a ball. Finally I give them a few instructions and they make a few short sprints. I do not say much to the players, I simply observe them. Who looks to be in good form, and who looks uncomfortable? When we leave the field I pat a few players on the shoulder if I think they need encouragement. There is always a feeling of tension before a match, this is essential, and the players should feel it too. You can tell during the warming-up whether the tension is there.

Half Time

You come in and you tell the players to sit down quietly. You ask who needs treatment. You let them get their breath and then you start to talk. You deal with the main points and say a few words about each individual. Then you explain what has to change, and what has to improve. If things are going well, you tell the players to remain alert and concentrated, and warn them about certain situations. For example, you remind them to retain their organization and discipline, and not to get over-confident. My talk has no definite length. Sometimes I finish quickly, and sometimes I am still speaking when the players have to go out again. The score does not determine what I say. You might be 1-0 down due to an unlucky goal, but otherwise be playing well. You could spend time talking about the goal, but there is not much point. Occasionally I read the riot act. Against NAC, for example, we started far too carelessly and fell 1-0 behind. However, in general I find it ridiculous that you should have to motivate players who play for PSV at this level. They are doing this for themselves! Players have to prove themselves. I have offered to give individual coaching outside the obligatory training sessions. I also tell the players that I do not want to hear their gripes at the end of the season.

Coping with One Player Down

Recently we played against Club Bruges. Our central midfielder was sent off. I decided to switch our right midfielder to the center, because he stimulates the team to play good soccer. With ten men we turned a 1-0 deficit into a 2-1 lead. We started to pass the ball around at the moment when the Bruges players began to run with the ball. The 11 players often think that they have to run less because they have one man more. Often it is as though the ten players have more room, or the space that they have is exploited better.

Do you ever explain to the squad why you made a substitution?
No. If the players do not ask, then I assume they understand why. You have to avoid talking too much. You cannot discuss everything. The squad can also take the initiative occasionally. I have never known the players to come and ask me questions. Except once, when they asked me why we were not playing man-to-man to deny our opponents space. I explained that you cannot keep doing this when you lose every game. However, playing man-to-man for a short time during a match is a good way of finding out what is

going wrong. You can see which players are not winning their duels and, therefore, where you need to intervene.

Post Game Analysis

Usually I take five or ten minutes before the first coaching session after the match to tell the players my views on the match. The players also get the chance to air their opinions. Unfortunately the first team players who take part in the match are training with the first team, so I can never get my whole team together. I explain in general what the team did well and what went wrong, sometimes with references to specific players. I might say, "You have to watch out for that," or "In this situation, that went wrong," or "You have to do that better," or "Why did you not do that?" You can also deal with a few aspects of the game during the half-time break. I never say much immediately after a match. If the players were not trying hard enough, or their movement was poor, I might give them a dressing down. These are signs that their attitude was wrong, and that is unacceptable. You simply have to react. Otherwise I limit myself to a few minor aspects after a match. I might quietly approach a player and ask why he did not pass the ball square to a teammate who was in a better position at a certain moment. If he answers that he did not hear anyone call for the ball, I go the other player and ask why he did not call. That sort of thing. I deal with everything else on the next day. On the evening after a match you are often exhausted - you are just empty. Nevertheless the coaching staff always discusses the game briefly while relaxing with a glass of beer.

I can see whether things are going well after just ten minutes of a game. During the game I see what goes wrong. These are things that I mention during the break. I have a helper to write everything down, because it is impossible to remember everything. I do not write anything myself because I may miss something of importance by taking my eyes off the game. During the evening I think about the match, but in general the same aspects always come to the fore and maybe a few additional thoughts occur, but in general I already have everything in my head.

Inherent Problems for the Coach of the 2nd Team

The players know the tasks and functions associated with each position. If a striker has always listened carefully, then he knows what he has to do if he has to play at left-half on occasion. Naturally you always talk to your players before a match. For example, Ayaz usually plays as a striker and is therefore used to taking a direct route towards goal down the center of the pitch. If he has to play left-half, then I tell him to use the wing, and to spread the play wide. Sometimes the team is completely unbalanced. For example, in an away game against NAC my team consisted of one defender and ten attackers. With so many attackers in our team, we had to ensure that we scored more goals than the opposition, because we simply could not rely on our defense. We created a lot of goal scoring chances, but we made too many defensive mistakes and thus we lost. I had strikers who were forced to play in right and left midfield. There were also first team players who needed to improve their fitness. Faber at right-back, for example, and Van de Weerden in front of the defense. Obviously the first team always has priority, and the second team has to adjust accordingly. The second team is also there for players who have been injured or out of form. All of the players who appear in the second team are discussed every two weeks with Advocaat, Arnesen and Bruins Slot.

Coaching Strikers from Game Situations

The composition of the second team frequently varies, so using incidents from the match as a basis for coaching sessions can be a problem. For example, recently I wanted to coach my defense in playing against two strikers and against three strikers, simply to go over a number of aspects again. Suddenly my central defender was taken away to train with the first team. I coach my players in aspects of the game that went wrong; things like controlling a pass, or crossing, or running off the ball. In particular the runs made by the strikers - they are not direct enough, and they need to alternate with more one-twos. Our play down the center of the pitch could be better. The players should not stand in a straight line down the center but should learn to position themselves slightly offset from the others. I coach these specific aspects because they go wrong during matches. So the second team does not just practice general drills. The younger players in particular need to improve. They have to learn how to cope with situations on the pitch. I insist on this. I hate it when strikers simply turn with the ball without knowing who is behind them. They simply turn and as a result the defender takes the ball from them. A player with a marker behind him must lay the ball off and move. After the lay-off he must be ready to receive the ball again. You can coach this specifically. The moment when the coach intervenes is also important. For example, the ball is thrown in

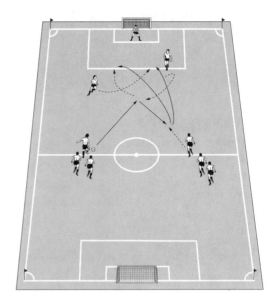

ex. Offensive Patterns

to a player. When the ball reaches him the coach shouts, "Lay it off!" This is too late. The instruction has to come when the throw-in is taken. That is when the player has a yard of space, and that is what is important.

My striker always calls for the ball too early. A striker first needs to get into the final third of the pitch, behind the back of his marker. He has to maintain visual contact with the ball carrier and then call for the ball. If he is in space he can turn, and if not he should lay the ball off and sprint away from his marker. These are the essentials. If one striker drops deeper, the other should go forward and exploit the space beyond the first striker. You tell your players these things hundreds of times, and you practice them in patterns. I covered this in my examination to become a professional soccer coach. Play the ball into a square, lose your marker and make a run, and link up. You can put two genuine strikers in the attacking positions if you want to coach them specifically, but you can also rotate your players. Let the man who plays the ball take over the striker's position later. It is important that each player concentrates on what the others are doing, and that they time their runs well. You can introduce an element of resistance by working with defenders, but I do not do this very often. The pitch has to be very good, and because the defenders know what is going to happen, their task is too easy. So I often dispense with defenders. Naturally you let the strikers play alongside each other in positional and small sided games, and you expect to see them use the runs they have practiced.

Developing Drills

Sometimes new drills and small sided games are developed through necessity because of the numbers or types of players at practice. Recently I wanted to work on players taking up positions slightly offset from each other. I had intended to use a specific drill but because I had twelve players rather than eleven, I immediately thought, 'That is four plus four plus three.' So I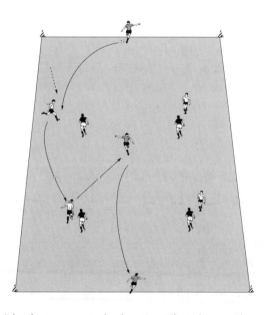
played four against four with three neutral players. The three players were positioned down the middle of the pitch, with one of them at each end. The players at each end had to stay there. The neutral players were always on the side of the team that had possession. The player in possession could only touch the ball twice. The game was thus seven against four. The point of the game is to stay in position and keep shape. When one player goes towards the ball, the other must not follow him, but must look for a clear passing line. Before the player receives the ball he has to know who he is going to pass it to. I insist that the players first assess whether they can play the ball forward. Forward passes should always take priority over square passes. The aim is to keep possession for as long as possible. So the players have to form triangles, play the ball to each other under knee height, keep their distance from each other, move in response to each other's movements, and think ahead. If things go

well, give some of the players the task of touching the ball only once when in possession - for example, if one of the strikers spends too much time on the ball. This is a tiring drill, if you play it properly. You can introduce a competitive element by making the team that does not have the ball in the last minute do 25 push-ups. This stimulates the players to chase the ball and provide maximum resistance, just as in a real match. The specific aspect is that the sides of the pitch must be manned by players who occupy the flanks during a real match. The three neutral players also play frequently down the middle of the pitch in my team.

The System of Play

We always play 4:4:2. Of course, you often know how your opponents will play. Heerenveen, for example, plays with three strikers. Sometimes you might decide to take out a central defender and replace him with a midfielder who will play just in front of the defense. This means changing your usual organization, but sometimes that is necessary to allow the team to function better. But

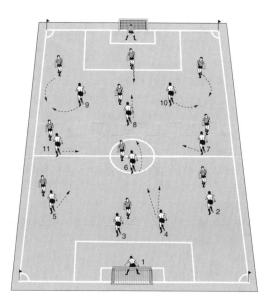

usually we play 4:4:2, just like our first team. I have the freedom to make changes during the match. I also have the freedom to decide whether or not to play a pressing game. We pressured Ajax, for example, from the kick-off. That worked well. We held our own for the first 30 minutes and even took a 1-0 lead. Mistakes allowed Ajax to score two goals and we were then unable to recover.

During the pre-game talk we refer to the system of play and agree what to do about it. In this case we agreed to mark the Ajax players closely. We wanted to disrupt their buildup play. We wanted to set

them under pressure immediately. Our numbers 2, 3 and 5 marked the three Ajax strikers. Numbers 7 and 11 had to cover their left half and right half. This means that numbers 4 and 6 then have to work well together.

If number 6 marks Ajax's number 10, number 4 can go forward. On another occasion number 4 does the marking and number 6 can go forward. This depends on the players' abilities, and can vary from game to game. Numbers 9 and 10, our strikers, have to push closer together when Ajax's sweeper has the ball. If they are too far apart, number 8 can push forward to cover the sweeper. This means that numbers 4 and 6 must also push forward. But, in principle, 9 and 10 must push towards the ball. If the right-back has possession, number 9 goes towards him and number 10 covers the center. If this is not possible, number 8 must block the full-back's forward run.

There are often problems with the strikers. They are all attacking types - Claudio, Ayaz, Pjotr - and are of different nationalities. We agree that they should fall back to the edge of the center circle and exert pressure on the flank where the opposition is trying to build up a move. If the right-back makes a forward run, the number 9 - if he is nearest - must move towards him, while number 10 covers his back and number 8 goes to help them. If the sweeper has the ball, we have to wait and see. If he moves forward, go to challenge him on the edge of the center circle. Everyone tends to move towards the middle. But what happens when the game is 10 minutes old? Number 9 goes and challenges the opposition's sweeper. I shout to him, 'What did we agree?' This sort of thing still surprises me. Brazilians like Claudio play purely by instinct. It is then difficult to say exactly what they should do.

The Opposition

You often know how a club's second team will play, because they operate the same system as the club's first team. You don't know all the players. Those who appear regularly in the first team are, of course, familiar. Nygaard, the striker who played for MVV last season and was previously with Heerenveen, is very dangerous in the air. He pushes and pulls, and is an excellent target man. Gorter of NAC is a playmaker. You have to avoid giving him time and space on the ball, and ensure that he has no opportunities to shoot from distance. You have to mark him closely and avoid giving away free kicks in dangerous positions. Obviously you warn your team about these aspects. On the other hand, you do not know who will be playing until shortly before the match. Nor am I sure that the players take in everything that they are told. When the game is in progress, I see things that make me wonder if a player has been listening to what I say. But I was sometimes like that, too, when I was a player. It is understandable. Players are only human. The players do take in much of what you say, but you have to repeat yourself sometimes. A coach wants his players to think just as he does. It does not matter how he achieves this, as long as the players understand him. I try to do this by coaching situations as they arise. I frequently stop the drill and explain the situation to the players.

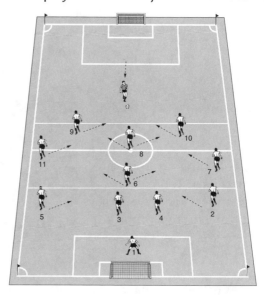

Coaching the Under 16 Team

The team is made up of 14 year old players, and has only won twice so far. The opposing players are all 15. At a certain moment I realized that I was treating the youths in the same way as PSV's second team players. I then told them that they should tell me if I was too hard on them. No one objected - the players even said that they had the impression that they were really learning something. I enjoy my work with the under 16 team, which takes up my Tuesday and Thursday evenings, and sometimes Saturdays, when I can make it. It is a pleasure to see how keen they are and how quickly they learn.

The drills are sometimes the same as for PSV's second team. For example, I use a positional game of four against four, with four lay-off players on the sidelines, with both Unitas and PSV. The A players ask the B players which positions are occupied, or in other words which positions they can pass the ball to. "Left, right, in front, behind," is the answer. This is how they learn. At PSV they go into more detail, of course. You introduce higher levels of resistance, and you look more at the possible passing lines and the distances between the players but the pattern remains the same. How do we play when we have possession, when we lose possession and when possession changes? When we have possession we try to get the ball to the strikers as soon as possible. We play 4:4:2 with a diamond shape in midfield. I emphasize linking up between the lines and creating space. When we lose the ball our two central defenders closely mark the opposing team's two strikers. If the opposition has one central striker, a defender takes up a position either in front of or behind him. The players are all younger, so covering play is often more important. When we lose possession everyone has to get back into position as soon as possible and close down the available space. We always discuss taking restart plays, corners and defending

against them and how to organize our defensive wall at free-kicks, this is very important.

Scouting the 1st Team's Opponents

It is important to see what formation the team plays in, and what its strengths and weaknesses are. And naturally you want to know the individual skills of the players. Which players dictate the play and will therefore have to be carefully watched? What are the players' specific strengths? Restart plays are also very important. Recently I saw the match between the Czech and Slovak international youth teams, the result was 3-2 and four of the five goals resulted from restart plays. There are therefore a lot of possibilities. Dick Advocaat, our head coach, always wants to know everything about PSV's next opponent. Restart plays and buildup patterns are especially important. If you know, for example, that Koeman dictates the buildup play for Groningen, then you ensure that he cannot do this against PSV. If you know that an opposing goalkeeper is not very good at kicking the ball when it is on the ground, then you force the opposing players to pass the ball back frequently to him. Lots of details. Advocaat knows how RKC plays, but he does not see them every week. So it is important that someone goes to observe them before we play against them.

During the last 20 years there has been a revolution in match preparation and knowledge of opponents. Everything is more detailed. Everything is approached more analytically. Everything is sifted through. Videotapes are used, and specific situations are looked at time and again. When we played Dynamo Kiev in the Champions League their players knew everything about PSV.

Before the game, Advocaat frequently told us that Kiev had a good, young team, and that we could not afford to underestimate them. Look at how the Ukraine performed in the World Cup qualification games, Croatia beat them for the final spot in a play off and eight or nine Kiev players were in the national team. Kiev's buildup play is very good. But I think that the team made the best possible use of the chances it had. I saw Kiev play against Newcastle. It created ten chances and only converted two. Against us it only created five chances, but scored from three of them. PSV also had a number of chances and only took one. That was the big difference. We know that Kiev can play well. The players can all hit a good long or short pass, and they are all fast, nimble and athletic. The two strikers are 'murderers,' who can switch perfectly between attack and defense. This was all known and we took measures to deal with them. But their yield was sixty percent and ours was only ten percent. That was the difference. Newcastle scored two lucky goals against Kiev. That's soccer. And that's the attraction of soccer. In my opinion, PSV played well against Kiev. As well as it could, in any case. If you are all in top form and you play with this amount of commitment, then you win a game like that. But players are not robots. One week they play well, and the next less so.

CHAPTER 8

The Match As Seen Through the Eyes of the Amateur Coach: Karel Hiddink

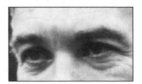

Karel Hiddink is the coach of Rheden, a top-level amateur club. After a career as a professional soccer player with FC Groningen, Veendam and De Graafschap, he took the post of assistant coach of De Graafschap in Doetinchem, where he was the right-hand man of Pim Verbeek and Simon Kistemaker. He then went into amateur soccer, where he spent one season as head coach to amateur club Varsseveld, and three seasons with HSC'21 in Haaksbergen. At the moment he is in his second season at Rheden. Hiddink gives us his views on various aspects of match analysis:

Hiddink: I make notes during the match and look for aspects of the game that I can refer to during the break. After the match I also record a few things briefly, and I try not to be distracted by my emotions. You cannot afford to be, especially if you are facing the press. Next day, when you see your words in the newspapers, it is too late to be sorry for what you said.

I do not talk to the players in detail after a match, I wait until the following evening when we have a training session. I talk about the main aspects of the match and discuss with the squad whether the things

we spoke about before the match were in fact put into practice. Depending on the weather, I might do this in the locker room or on the pitch.

During the discussions before and after a match, I use a magnetic board and small magnets. When I talk to specific individuals on their own, I have a smaller magnetic board available. This helps me to make certain situations clearer. I also find it important to let the players say what they thought of the match. There must be an exchange of ideas between the players and the coach.

There is a consistent theme running through my training sessions. If something goes wrong during a match, it is not the case that the following sessions are completely devoted to this. Training sessions always include important aspects that constantly recur. When you join a club, you make a list of the technical abilities of the players, how well they can control the ball, their movement off the ball, etc. These are the things you work on, they form the basis for your training sessions, and you return to them again and again.

This does not mean that I do not refer to the match. For example, a player might make too few runs to create space for others. Players make runs mainly because they want to receive the ball themselves. However, they should try to think one step further. I see this constantly, so I create drills to practice these situations.

We start to work towards the next match on the day after the last game. It is good that we have a training session then. This is certainly true if the team has lost - you can draw a line under the defeat and look forward.

I always gather information about our next opponent. We have a relatively small staff, so there is no one who can go to watch our next opponents. However, I am already familiar with a lot of clubs, and I try to keep up to date through all kinds of other channels (newspaper articles, for example). The system of play - whether the team plays with two or three strikers - is especially important.

Above all, we try to play our own game. Nevertheless, some opponents do have specific characteristics, and I coach the team accordingly. For example, I knew that an opposing team was very slow down the center of the pitch, and I coached my team to exploit this. Our two strikers covered the flanks when our opponents had the ball, so that their buildup had to take place down the center, where our two attacking midfielders formed a defensive block. We practiced this in training sessions, and it worked well during the match.

However, I rarely adjust the team to take account of our opponents. I prefer to rely on our own strengths. I work to a specific concept with the squad, and I always try to expand on this during my coaching.

Apart from their system of play the mental attitude of the opponent is also important. If a potential championship winning team loses three successive games, it is important to know how their players cope. You have to try to exploit this by ensuring that you hit them early in the game to increase their problems.

I tell the team who is playing ninety minutes before the match. I leave it this late because a lot can happen between the final training session and the match. However, I try to keep a fairly stable team. I talk things over with my assistant coach, but I choose the team myself. The team captain also has no influence. In effect, no one else influences the selection process. Obviously you come up against people who have their own ideas, but I am the one who decides on the lineup. That is clearly regulated in my job description. Even the club's administrators cannot interfere. Their job is in the boardroom.

Pre-match discussion

First, I talk about the defensive tasks. I tell the players who they can expect to face and about the opposing team's specific characteristics - whether it tries to build up moves from the back, or to reach the strikers directly. Then we look at our defensive organization at restart plays such as free-kicks and corners - who has to stand where, etc.

I then focus on aspects that went wrong in the previous match. Although we have already mentioned these things in the post-match discussion, I refer to them again. Then we turn to the buildup and attack and I always try to explain why the players have to do certain things. Then I point out the specific characteristics of my team. To some extent a pre-match discussion involves repeating things that the players have already heard, but I think it is important to do this because the players tend to forget things in their enthusiasm when they are on the pitch.

Pre-match routine

I regard it as important that we depart punctually for away games and I always ensure that we have a margin of safety in case something goes wrong. I aim to be at the site of the match 90 minutes before kick-off, for both home and away games. If we have a long bus journey, we always stop somewhere along the route to stretch our legs. When we arrive, the trainer and the assistant have plenty of time to get everything and everyone ready for the match.

I always take a look at the players in the locker room when there is time to make any minor individual adjustments if anyone is not feeling well or an injury is bothering him. Sometimes I might have to relax the tension, and on other occasions the players might be too light-hearted and I will need to make them focus on the task at hand. I often leave the players on their own, so that they can talk things over without the coach being present.

The Warm-up

Between 30 and 35 minutes before the match we go outside to warm up. This is a gradual warming-up under the leadership of the captain. The players loosen up for a period of ten minutes. The squad stays together during these exercises. Then the ball is introduced. Groups of players from the various lines carry out a few passing drills. Each group decides the details for itself. One player might want to receive high balls that he has to jump for, while another may prefer to receive passes to his feet. The goalkeeper warms up separately with the reserve goalkeeper.

Towards the end of the warming-up period the players carry out a few faster exercises with the ball to round things off, turning quickly and accelerating. Finally there are two sprints with acceleration and the whole group goes back to the locker room.

The Substitutes

I try to keep a fairly constant basic team, the players know this and so I do not have to explain to players why they have or have not been picked each week. If, during the week, I decide to drop a regular player, then I let him know in due time.

I never promise a reserve that he will be brought on during a match. That just arouses expectations that you cannot always fulfill. What happens if the match does not go as expected? I prefer not to arouse false hopes and make promises that I cannot keep.

Naturally it is understandable that players do not want to be a substitute week after week. They want to play. This is a problem for all coaches at every level. It is not good for a soccer player to sit on the sidelines every week. However, the players I choose as substitutes must always be prepared to be brought on, they do not have any other tasks, such as fetching the ball. I let them warm up for five minutes when I intend to make a tactical substitution. I tell the substitute that he has five minutes to get ready. Sometimes you expect that certain players will have fitness problems towards the end of a match. So you let players warm up just in case this happens. If the weather is cold I let the players warm up so that they do not have to sit on the bench with cold feet, or come on cold as a substitute if suddenly needed.

I do not recommend making quick, early substitutions but you cannot always avoid it. A substitution must improve the situation, otherwise it is not worth making. Sometimes you have to let players carry on when they are not doing well, so that they can get over their bad patch. One successful move or play may be enough to get them back on track.

The reserves warm up before a match and during half time, but not very intensively. It is important that they keep warm and keep their focus on the game.

When a player comes off I usually do not have much time to explain why. Afterwards I tell the group why I made a tactical substitution. For instance, a team that usually plays with two strikers recently fielded three in a match against us. At first we had problems, and our left flank came under a lot of pressure. After about 20 minutes I made a substitution, bringing in a left-footed midfielder. This restored the balance of our team.

Coaching from the sideline

It is important not to become emotional on the sideline. During a match I am usually my normal self. Just after a match I sometimes take a step back before I face a confrontation. That has a refreshing effect. As I already mentioned, you do not want to read your words in the newspaper the next day with regret or say something to a player which will damage their confidence. As a player I used to hate it when a coach came out with unconsidered statements. Especially when things had not gone well.

Half time

At half time if we are losing I try to put things right. If we are winning I try to make the players aware of certain things. I tell them
what the opposition might do, and how they should react.

If a player does not carry out his tasks, or has a poor attitude, I
point this out to him as this is not acceptable. In these circumstances I might raise my voice. Otherwise I just remain as I am, I
never act or overreact. Motivation has to come from the players
themselves, and, fortunately, that is the case at Rheden.

After the match

When the game is over I always keep the referee in view. Players can
react very emotionally, so I always watch him in case he needs help.
I might be angry with the referee myself, but I never show this. As
coach I have to set an example. After a match I go into the locker
room with the team, though occasionally I might sit by myself to
think things through first.

Criticism from outside

My primary concern is the players, they are important, how they are
playing, how they are feeling and developing as a unit. Naturally I
am prepared to listen to criticism but only from people who know
what they are talking about. I am always approachable. However, I
rarely talk about specific players. That only happens sporadically,
and then I usually speak positively about them.

CHAPTER 9

The Match As Seen Through the Eyes of a Belgian Coach: Danill de Paepe

A strong wind in blowing is Hamme, a village in East Flanders. A few supporters are huddled together on the edge of the practice pitches. The local club, VW Hamme, plays in the Belgian second division and has known better times. It faces a difficult season with a small squad of 15 average players.

And yet the atmosphere at the club is relaxed. Through good times and bad, Hamme remains a family club, with magnificent supporters. A club built on the unpaid efforts of willing helpers. A club that eats, drinks and makes merry. This is the strength of Hamme, a club united, come what may. The strength of the club is personified above all in its 50-year-old coach, Daniĺl de Paepe. De Paepe, the production manager of a plastics processing company, has coached the club for eight years. A difficult combination, but it is made easier by the helpfulness of the people of Hamme.

De Paepe: I come here straight from my office. After the training session my meal is ready, prepared for me by the people here. These are values that are expressed not in money but in feelings, and that is very important for me.

No one can spoil this mood, even on this Monday, with the club near the bottom of the league and yet another defeat behind it. And what a defeat - 1-7 in Waregem! An absolute drubbing for all Hamme fans. This must be a new low point.

I have not yet analyzed the Waregem game together with the players. I do not do that on the day of the game, because my judgement is often still clouded by my emotions. Usually I wait until Friday, and then I start the first pre-match discussion with a review of the last match. If things have gone really badly, then I make an exception and we discuss the game on the Monday evening, because everything is still fresh in our minds. 7-1 was a bad result, but I want to talk things over calmly with the management committee. I have thought everything through clearly in my mind. Whether I put pen to paper depends on the match and, of course, the result. I will discuss the situation with the whole squad. I do discuss our problems with individual players, but experience has taught me that this does not shed a lot of light on the situation. If we concede too many goals, the players always put forward different reasons. For example, we play too offensively or too defensively, we should play down the flanks more, we play too centrally. A player's explanation always depends on whether he feels threatened, or whether his position in the team is endangered.

If individuals have made mistakes, I take them aside during a training session. I do this on Thursdays. Briefly and always on the pitch itself - never between these four walls. My assistant supervises the drills and everyone can see that I talk things over with a certain player without resorting to angry gestures or shouting. I try to ensure that this does not become a set pattern. Sometimes I single out a player who has done well, and sometimes I take the whole central backbone of the team to one side, or the defensive line. We try to vary things.

Review

Last Friday, two days before the game against Waregem, I reviewed the match against Geel, our previous opponent. That game ended in a 1-1 draw. I started by pointing out that we had not achieved our objective. We wanted to win against Geel, and we wanted to introduce a new system of play. We had been unable to keep a clean sheet because we played too offensively. So we assumed that we would go through the 90 minutes without conceding a goal. 'And we will make sure that we score a goal. That means we will win and gain three points.' My message was that simple. How we did it, and whether we played attractive soccer or not, was irrelevant. All that counted was the points. The way we play is secondary. Thirdly I want to involve as many players as possible. And fourthly I want to see as many goals as possible. But we have a long way to go. Last year, in the third division, that was all very logical, but now we have other, more important worries. However, going back to our objective, we had not achieved it. Firstly, and above all, we could not avoid conceding a goal. The main reason for this - and you have to tell your players this - was because there were too many individual mistakes. It would be wrong to point a finger at anyone directly, so you do not name any names. For example, the goalkeeper dropped the ball. They all know that themselves, and they know who I am talking about. Secondly I admit that we had problems adjusting to the existing system. I say that to soften the blow, because I have criticized them. Now I admit that I can understand their problems to some extent. Thirdly I point out that we have not made use of our chances. The reason? We reacted too late; we were not alert enough. If the opposing goalkeeper drops the ball, this is when my players start to move. This is too late - they should anticipate these things and be in position to exploit them. You cannot criticize anyone personally for this. On another day we will get three chances and score from all of them. You cannot do anything about this. Of course, if you regularly create ten chances and do not score from any of them, then you have a problem.

I am just looking through the list that I drew up after the game against Geel. Sometimes these are just small points, things that everyone knows, but are frequently neglected. Two players going for the same ball, for instance. Again, we worked hard to win the ball, but then we passed it badly. That sort of thing does not help our game. I could go on and on. We play with too many men in front of the ball. In our league you usually find the opposite - almost every team plays with too many men behind the ball. Eight players behind the ball and only two in front.

Outlook

On Friday evening I only talk about our opponents, and never about my own team. I save that for the day before the match. After discussing the previous game, I talk about the future. We did not achieve our objective, so we will have to do something about this. We will have to learn to keep a clean sheet. Everyone must be able to play with this in mind. I have to choose my words carefully, because if I say that we are going to play more defensively, there will be an immediate reaction from the more attack-minded players. They do not like the idea. I also make no secret of the fact that a multifunctional player will soon arrive. The squad can get used to the idea that a new player will turn up for a trial. Thirdly I try to convince the players that we will win some points in the next few games. We won a point at Ostende, for example - a club that was at the top of the league at the start of the season. We could just as easily have won or lost. In every game we could have won, but every time that we did not lose, we could just as easily have done so. It was always a close-run thing.

I coach the team on Friday with an eye to the match on the coming Sunday. I am mindful of our opponents - for example, Waregem. Devreese is very fast, and Calo is strong and mobile. I take account of this in the drills, and of Waregem's strong play down the flanks. The players are not aware of this. A soccer player does not come to a training session to think. Take the example of the match against Turnhout. Turnhout plays with a lot of men behind the ball, so when possession is lost it is important to switch over to defense. Unfortunately our players stood 5 yards from their immediate opponents when we had the ball, and the same distance when we did not. You can switch to defense by running, by switching from walking or standing still to a sprint to get back into a defensive position. But persuading a soccer player to sprint for a negative objective is difficult. They might sprint after a rolling ball, but give them the task of sprinting back for no better reason than to take up a defensive position, and you have a problem. So today we occupied ourselves with competitive games in which two players suddenly had to sprint to another pitch. The players do not know that this is in preparation for Sunday. This opens up opportunities for me. For example, the drill went well the first three times, but the fourth time there was less effort. That also happens during a match, so I was able to focus on this. I tell them that their concentration is less the fourth time, and that is when we concede a goal. I can prove it to them, and then they are more ready to accept it. I have to admit that, with our limited number of training sessions, we can only achieve a 30% return from this sort of drill. Our training schedule is light conditioning for one hour on Monday, with a little physical training. Other clubs can focus on the medical treatment of their players, (massage, sauna, light recuperation run), but we do not have the facilities, so we cannot do any of these things. On Tuesdays the emphasis is on physical conditioning, with the first team and the reserves together. This might be a pattern of pure running exercises or a competitive drill with one against one. Wednesday is a day off. On Thursday we practice match situations and finishing, and play a practice match, sometimes with the team that will start on Sunday and sometimes not. For my part, the first team players do not always have to be on the winning side. Excessive enthusiasm can reduce my already limited squad still further. On Friday we deal with theory, and fine-tune our restart plays and routine moves. We have our own patterns of play. We discuss them at the start of the season, and every player must learn them. By September they should be familiar with them, and now we just need to perfect them. Another problem is that I always have to hold the training sessions on the B pitch, and that is very different from the A pitch, where there are no lights. These are all details that do not make my work any easier. I do not have a wall, for example. I have to ask my players to set up a wall so that my free-kick specialist can practice. Otherwise I have to let him practice with the goalkeeper and then do other drills with the main group in the intervals. But we manage.

Some coaches work out everything down to the tiniest details. This is true during training sessions as well. They tell the players how many yards they have run and in how many minutes. But players do not come to coaching sessions to think - you have to keep them busy so that they run for miles without being aware of it. I regularly test them over 400 or 600 yards, or give them a Cooper test, but it should not turn into an athletics competition. I am not interested in finding out who is the best. But I want to see the player who ended in last position the previous time finish next to last this time. I often schedule running drills at the end of the training session. That is not logical, and most coaches carry out these drills after intensive warming up at the start of a session. My reasons are psychological - in the locker room the players have the feeling that they have worked better and more intensively after they have been made to sweat. This is different to finishing with cooling down. Cooling down is fine for full professionals, but we do not have any. Everyone has a job until four or five p.m., then they come to the training session, and they do not get home until ten or eleven o'clock. Those are long days. Waregem's players have training sessions at 10 a.m. and 3 p.m. They are finished before our players even start. We have training sessions four days a week, and this is too often for some of the players. What should I do? Tell them that we will only train on three days, as we did last season? That might be less stressful, but you do not change things just to suit someone who cannot meet the demands at this level. Other players need four sessions. Moreover we have no foreign players. That is also something unique.

Observing the opposition

After the review of the previous match, it is time to talk about our next opponent. In this case, Waregem. I always do that on Friday evening. I talk about the team solely on the basis of reports made by my assistant coach, Maurice Blommaert, together with Luc Mathys. They provide me with a file containing data about the team, the system of play, the lineup, the shape, the numbers, who is left-footed and who is right-footed, their restart plays, etc. I read the file closely beforehand. The first page gives the regular eleven and the players' positions, and the positional changes associated with substitutions. Then the observer describes the match, because the atmosphere around a match can change completely from one visit to the next. He draws his conclusions from all these elements.

He then makes a few useful comments, such as who has a long throw-in, who takes over the sweeper's position when the sweeper goes forward, etc. He also analyzes every player in detail, even the substitutes. Take Jude Vandelannoitte, for example: a left winger, who likes to move infield with the ball at his feet; sometimes takes the ball too far; does not vary his pace very often; not very good defensively; good striker of the ball with his left foot; fairly good technique; very offensive; difficult to part from the ball. Everything is there in black and white. This report tells you everything you need to know if you have to face this player. My team knows that this is largely Maurice's work, not mine, and this reinforces his authority when he is in charge of a training session. Lots of coaches never mention the people who analyze other teams for them, but it is not my style to make use of someone else's work without any acknowledgement.

Risk

After the analysis of the opposing players the restart plays are described - corners and free-kicks, for and against, as well as short corners and special plays - and the goals. I hang this up later in the locker room, usually on the day of the match. This page also describes who appears at the near post and the far post, who takes up position to receive the ball from a short corner or free-kick, who heads the ball on, and other variations. When the drawings are hung up, they show who is going to play against whom. Obviously this is all in vain if I do not know the opposition's lineup. I am therefore taking a big risk. Fortunately Waregem started as I had anticipated. But that is not always the case and you have to use your head. You have to know which team your opponents last played against, and whether they won or lost. Our opponents always play against KV Mechelen one week before they play us. That can be a disadvantage. Mechelen is one of the favorites to win the league, and does not lose very often. As a consequence, our next opponents often make changes to the team before playing us. This is difficult to predict. Waregem lost 0-1 to Mechelen, but was not outclassed, so I assumed that the team would not be changed.

Then we come to the day of the match. The opposition's line up is displayed on a large sheet of paper, with a short description of each player's main characteristics under his name. These have already been discussed on the Friday evening. There is also a photo of the opposing team. The players can refresh their memories. Then I leave the team to get on with it. Besides the names of my players and their opponents, the board also shows a number of important symbols, which only insiders can understand. For example, we always form a four-man wall. The names of the four players are underlined. The player who takes the corners has an asterisk against his name. The players who form a two-man wall are indicated by two asterisks (in practice the center-forward always drops back on the right or left flank). Penalties are taken by the player with P1 against his name. If he is injured or substituted, P2 takes over. A vertical dotted line indicates the player who has to sprint towards the ball when a free-kick is taken against us. These symbols save me a lot of time during discussions on theory. In addition, I do not have to make many corrections on the field - I don't have to keep jumping up and running to the sideline to shout instructions to the players. The players already know what to do. If you have to organize these things just before the match, then you have not done your work properly during the previous week. We regulate these things before the season starts. This makes your work easier, and you have more time to focus on the match. And that is what is important.

In the run-up to the match I go through the most important

points concerning our opponents. For example: big players; slow in defense, but strong; inswinging crosses. All short phrases, just notes on my piece of paper, but you string them together into a logical report. In modern soccer the smallest details make all the difference between winning and losing. Emphasizing these things week by week does not automatically guarantee success. No way. Before the match against Waregem I also told my players that we were facing a counterattacking team, and that we should play the ball along the ground because we have a lot of small players. Keep things as tight as possible to give ourselves a good chance of keeping a clean sheet. Do not let Waregem's two strikers, Devreese and Calo, into the game. I emphasize that we need 100% concentration for 90 minutes. But what happens? Devreese and Calo create the first two goals, and we are completely overrun.

The word "referee" is also on my list. That is to say, we are playing away, so be careful what you do. But what happens at the start of the match? Pascal de Labbeke mistimes a tackle and is given a red card, so we have to play on with only ten men. The way things happen sometimes has nothing to do with what you have told the players.

The match

We ensure that we are always at the ground 90 minutes before the match starts. Preferably after a bus journey that has not been too much of a strain on the nerves. This means that we should arrive on time, the heating should not be turned up unless we request it, the accompanying music should be suitable, etc. By the way, the players' wives ride with us. I have no objections. When we arrive we can take a quiet look at the pitch, or go for a short walk. This gives me time to talk. If there is a player who was in the team last week but not this, I take him aside and explain why he is not in the starting eleven. I think that he deserves an explanation. Of course, the discussion must always leave the player some degree of hope. At some stage I will have to give him a chance to prove that I was wrong to put him on the substitutes' bench. The players who are in the starting line-up are also informed beforehand. I announce the team very late because so much could still happen - injuries and so forth. The players probably know fairly accurately what the line-up will be on the basis of the training sessions, the theory talks and other minor matters. Incidentally, I have very little room for maneuver. I cannot introduce zonal defense because we do not have the right players for it. I only have two sturdy markers, who are not technically capable of playing in a zone. So they already know two of the team, assuming all the members of the regular squad are available.

Forty-five minutes before the match I start my talk. My assistant coach is in charge of the warming up, because everyone has to come to me again. I then discuss matters that have to be talked about man to man. Some players require tough talking, others have to be approached more gently, more psychologically. You cannot treat everyone in the same way. Sometimes you have to tell half truths. For example, I might tell a player that the opposition's coach has said that he is the weak link in our team. I motivate him by telling him that I am convinced that this is not the case, but he must prove it with his play. There are other players who cannot be talked to like this. Such an approach only works if you know your players well. If you succeed, the team's motivation is good, but after a hammering like yesterday's - I don't know. When we played Cercle Bruges I told Christaens that he was only in the team to play Lucas out of the game, and if he could do more than that, then I would regard it as a bonus. "But Lucas must not appear in the match, unless he is shown a red card of course," were my words. What happened? Christiaens set up our two goals. That was over and above his task, but he was also to blame for Lucas scoring a goal against us and being able to set up the equalizer. So he did not perform his task well. In such situations I never criticize a player by name during half time, but always deal with the team as a whole. The players know who is to blame when someone makes a bad mistake. You can occasionally become angry during a match, but then you really do have to be angry. It is no good just acting. The player will know when you do not mean it. It is pointless to shout at your players after each of 3 successive defeats. Of course, you cannot plan beforehand to be really angry. Anger has to overcome you. A lot of coaches do try to plan their outbursts. You hear them say, "I will get mad at them during half time, then things will get better." This does not work. I do not think that it has any effect, and I have always worked this way. I have been a coach for sixteen years - eight years at Evergem Center and eight years with VW Hamme. Why? Results, of course, and working on the basis of a long-term policy. Not from shouting and raging and pointing at others. That is a short-term approach. Coaches who work that way can give a brief boost to a team that is having a bad spell when they start to work with it, but the initial effect soon disappears. Having a big mouth is not my style, and I cannot change my ways. I am a very calm coach, I never lose control and I always look for psychological solutions to problems. I try to touch the right chord in a soccer player. I could send players home or suspend them, but that is a shortsighted policy. I could never have stayed at one club for eight years if I ruled with an iron fist.

Warming up

I prepare everything on the morning before the match. I write a lot, but everything has to be in my head as the match approaches. You can ask me anything - I will be able to answer perfectly. The big problem with coaches is that they think players take in everything as attentively as they themselves do. That is not the case. And then, the way in which the information is put over plays an important role. This is why the players must have a good idea of the opposition team in their heads on the Friday preceding the match.

Thirty minutes before the game each player starts on his warming-up, under the control of the assistant coach, to a fixed pattern that not everyone sees. We assume that each player will find his second wind. The players really have to raise a sweat before they come back to the changing room. Many players view warming up too simply, and do not take it seriously. They come back without having broken sweat and they are usually the ones who cannot put in that little bit of extra effort during the match. Warming up traditionally takes place across the pitch. We have done this with ball drills for a long time, but now you see teams increasingly playing various types of games.

During the match the reserve goalkeeper notes every important phase, just as a journalist would. This stops him from losing concentration, and I have proof of what happened if anyone denies it. In addition my assistant coach has a notebook, and writes down everything that I tell him. Comments such as, "He should get further forward," or "He should pass the ball sooner," or "He is standing too far away from his opponent." During half time I look at these notes and run through them again. I do not deal with everything. Some matters have already been corrected simply by calling out to the players during the match. My talk during half time differs from match to match. Do you start to speak immediately or leave the players to recover for five minutes? That depends on how the match is going. The players can exchange a few words with each other immediately. I let them do this, because they are playing into my hands. I wait until they arrive at the point that I want to discuss, and then I cut in. This is more effective. I ensure that I am always first into the locker room, so that I can see what sort of condition the players are in. The substitutes can stay outside. They know how things stand. Whether one of them will be brought on, or whether one of them should start to warm up. They know these things. Then there are a few "finer" points to discuss. The players must know which opponents have been shown a yellow card. Their numbers are written directly on the board. Why? Because they have to be shown a second yellow card as soon as possible! This brings us to the referee's role. The referee is only human. Pascal Devreese fooled the referee into giving one of our players a red card. I cannot be angry about it. He did it perfectly, and he was able to finish the game without difficulty. You have to teach your players to respect the referee. If he makes a mistake, for example, by awarding a cor-ner instead of a goal-kick, he may give us a free-kick for a slight push later in the game as a form of compensation. Provided you do not argue with him. After a match I am always last into the locker room because I try to be the first to congratulate the referee on his per-formance. I respect referees. But we were talking about the "finer" points. Another important point is the goal towards which a team plays. There is always a good end and a bad end, and you have to exploit this. Other details are the weather, and knowing whether a player has previously suffered an injury. Not that you should try to send him back to hospital, but the injury may be playing on his mind. Do not be a fool. Try to provoke something, because a play-er who retaliates will be sent off immediately. These are not things that you talk about in front of the whole team, but rather man to man.

Tactics

A quick substitution in the first half is not a good move, because then you are putting the blame for the team's bad performance onto the shoulders of one player. Unless you have told the player beforehand that, if the opposition does such and such, then we will have a problem, and in that case I will have to substitute you if things go badly. It can happen, and if it has to be done, then I do it. What happens more often is that you let a substitute warm up as a psychological measure, to stimulate a player who is on the pitch. Tactical interventions which turn out successfully are usually those that win a match, but which you do not boast about to the press. One example occurred during our away game at Ostende. I only had one striker. I could have played a midfielder as a second striker, but instead I elected to position a player behind the advanced striker. This was not our usual system, but we drew 0-0, which was a good result for us. I could have fielded the same team the next week, when my suspended second striker was available again, but I did not want to, because 0-0 is, after all, only 0-0, and does not really take you very far. And of course I would have had to sacrifice my second striker. We have so few strikers that it is asking for trouble to leave one on the bench. So I did the opposite of that which had brought me success. Anyway, a measure that is successful today will not necessarily be successful tomorrow. A coach intervenes a hundred times during a match, with little or no success. Just like a goalkeeper, who also makes various mistakes during a match, except that they must not decide the match. I attach a lot of value to superstition. The place where you always sit, the number you always wear, the route you take to the stadium. I used to count the red and green traffic lights, and this gave me an idea of the result in advance. Red was for our opponents, and green was for us. My players are the same. One of them always steps on a mat with his right foot first, another crosses himself, another always wears the same underpants - you are familiar with all the stories. I never say anything. I know how important these things are for the players.

Dialogue

I regularly talk to the three players who have all been team captain - Vergeylen, Ba and Stalpaert. They have to ensure that team spirit remains high, and that I hear about any problems. There is a technical staff of five, including myself. We work closely together, although there are always things that could be improved, of course

Immediately after the match I talk to the press. I spend a good two hours on the telephone. I take trouble to handle the press considerately. I always telephone reporters personally, in accordance with a fixed pattern. Even yesterday, after we lost 7-1, I still rang them. At home games, when reporters are usually present in person, I hold back. I prefer to let them talk to the players. After the game they can come into the locker room, because I know that they are not just looking for a sensational story. We can quietly sit and talk together after a training session or a match. After all, we are a family club.

CHAPTER 10

ANALYSIS OF THE '98 WORLD CUP

*J*an Rab traveled more than 5000 miles to observe and analyze *(potential) opponents of the Dutch team. His assistants are Ronald Spelbos and Nol de Ruiter. Part of his job is to gather all the data he can about opposing teams before he sees them, so that he will know what to look out for. When he looks back on the '98 World Cup, therefore, he does so as a well-informed commentator.*

Jan Rab: Surprisingly, I have read a number of very negative comments about this World Cup. That the play was too defensive; that the standard of play was poor; that there were no genuine stars, etc. I do not agree with these conclusions. I saw excellent games in a good atmosphere, and above all I saw superb soccer players. Michael Owen was the absolute number one. The best Dutch player was Edgar Davids, while the French had Zidane and Desailly. The young Argentinian, Gallardo, came on as a substitute and showed that he can become a great player. In fact, in every game I saw outstanding players. Even a country like Iran had a number of potential top players.

I think that some people confuse top players with old-fashioned stars, who could get by on the strength of just a few moments of genius. Players like that have almost disappeared from soccer at the highest level. I only saw one who falls into that category, and that was the Argentinian Ortega. After loss of possession his contribution was zero. But when his team had the ball, he was faster than anyone else to get into position to receive a pass. He devoted all of his energy to this, and he did it very cleverly. All of the other top players did their share of the work when the opposition had possession or there was a change of possession. Even Zidane was willing and able to defend. Owen has never known any other way of playing. Today's top players work for the team as a whole and not just for themselves.

Of the countries in the first four places, only Croatia played negatively. They relied heavily on their defense and their ability to get the ball quickly to Suker when they won possession. Virtually none of the other countries played defensively. Look at England and Argentina. It has been said that the Netherlands failed to reach the final because the team wanted to play too attractively. My response to that is to point to Italy. On the basis of his team's proven strengths, Maldini asked his players to take a much too careful and cautious approach. The result, Italy was knocked out of the tournament before the Netherlands.

To assess the tactical developments we have to look at the tournament's outstanding teams - France, the Netherlands and Brazil. Their defenders are capable of playing a zonal marking system. The two central defenders can read the game. Consider Frank de Boer and Jaap Stam, and how De Boer played against Ronaldo, for example. Standing off at the right moment, reading the direction of the attacker's run, and then stepping in to take the ball with apparent ease from the much faster player, purely on the basis of ability to read the game. The same applies to the French central defenders, Blanc and Desailly. They are not slow, but Blanc is certainly not the fastest of defenders. Because he reads the game so well, however, it is almost impossible to pass him.

The full-backs are skilled ball players. Their basic task is to defend, but they can participate in the buildup and attacking play without any difficulty. This means that they have to be fast and physically strong.

The player in front of the defense is perhaps the most important member of the team in modern soccer. The perfect example is the Brazilian, Dunga. He is responsible for maintaining the team's balance. He is the one who calls his colleagues to order if they disturb the team's balance by taking up the wrong position or losing possession unnecessarily. Such a controlling figure - the team's conscience, if you like - is absolutely essential. At the top level an organizational lapse will be punished immediately. Some teams had two players in front of the center of the defense. Brazil had Leonardo alongside Dunga. The cover they provided gave the full-backs, Cafu and Roberto Carlos, the opportunity to go forward. Players in this position must have two qualities. They must have a good overview of what is happening across the whole pitch, and they must be able to play in an extremely disciplined manner. I did not see Dunga leave his zone on a single occasion, even though the match situation was sometimes such that he must have been very tempted. France played with Deschamps and Petit alongside each other in front of the defense, although Deschamps played alone in this zone in the final. The system can vary, depending on the opposition.

The situation on the flanks also varied from opponent to opponent. Some teams played with an advanced midfielder in one game and a withdrawn midfielder in another. In the latter case the aim was to create space behind the opponent who was marking the withdrawn player.

Most teams played with two strikers. In most cases one of the strikers played as an advanced center-forward and the other, a more mobile striker, played off him.

A modern striker has to be willing to work hard. In this respect the work rate of Hernandez of Mexico and Batistuta of Argentina was fantastic. Personally I think that this should be the next step for Dennis Bergkamp. Dennis makes the team too vulnerable when it loses possession. Obviously he is a world-class player, but if he were willing to work harder for the team, he would be even more valuable.

During the course for professional coaches after the European Championships I was asked who would win the World Cup and predicted France. At that time the French had impressed me very much in England. Their defensive line was almost impassable, with a good goalkeeper behind it in Barthez. The midfield had all the necessary qualities - determination, work rate and creativity. There were problems with the strikers on the route to the final, and that is why Rinus Michels had doubts about France. It was known that AimÈ Jacquet

In the final, too, the French defense was impassible.

would have preferred to play with 3 strikers. France did not have 3 good strikers and that made the team vulnerable. The problem would not have been so serious if Dugarry had not been injured. He contributes a lot to the French style of play. He drags his marker or markers out of position and thus creates space for players like Zidane and Djorkaeff, who was one of the few French players who had a disappointing tournament. Given the above strengths of the team, together with its disciplined positional play, it was easy for me to tip France as the next world champion at an early stage.

The Germans were very disappointing. Their system of play, with a libero in the defensive line and another in midfield, is out of date. Then there were shortcomings on the flanks. There was often the appearance of a threat on the flank, but always from the same player, who had to cover immense distances. Moreover, after such a run down the wing the ball would often be played square or crossed too early. You have to hit crosses from the goal-line for good headers of the ball like Klinsmann and, in particular, Bierhoff. The Germans often hit their crosses from 20 yards out, and this makes life much easier for defenders. There were also weaknesses in the Germans' positional play. Of course, there are different ways of looking at soccer. During a coaching congress, Berti Vogts stated that, in his opinion, every youth team in Germany should play with 4 defenders. Later, in a personal discussion, it appeared that he assumed that one of the 4 would be a genuine sweeper, playing behind the others. In the Netherlands the sweeper plays in front of his co-defenders. That is another way of thinking. By the way, I am in favor of youth teams playing a zonal defense with four defenders. This makes it easier to build up the play from the back. When you have three defenders, they resort to long clearances too often. The team then has to try to win the ball when it breaks free from the resulting challenge. It is better for young players to learn how to build up moves from defense.

The pleasantest surprise? I found the first round to be less boring than during previous tournaments. I saw a lot of good teams whose play was a pleasant surprise - Paraguay, Iran and, in the same group as the Netherlands, Mexico. The Mexican coach always started too cautiously, but the team was capable of playing to a variety of concepts. Mexico started with one striker, but switched without difficulty to a system with 4 attackers. When I say "without difficulty," I mean that the team's organization remained sound. There was no reliance on pure chance. The team continued to play in a systematic and disciplined manner which is admirable.

I have to be careful what I say about the Netherlands!! I watched the team's opponents from the stands but I only saw the Dutch team's games on television and that is very different to watching from the stands. If you look back, we played the best soccer. Unfortunately we needed too many chances. It is typical that we only scored once from a counter-attack - Overmars against South Korea. The other goals all came from good buildup and attacking play. The team deserves to be complimented on this. No other team can match us in this respect. This underlines the Dutch team's cultured style of play, but how many more of the team's attacks should have resulted in goals? This is ultimately where we failed. We did not lose against Brazil in the penalty shoot-out but during the regular play, when we missed clear chances to score the winning goal.

I think that this is due to a lack of mental toughness on the part of the Dutch strikers rather than just bad luck. Take Kluivert against Croatia. A feint and then he hits the ball wrongly. "Wonderful feint - what a shame," we say. I disagree. Kluivert was in a position to score before he made the feint, so he should have tried to score immediately. If he had missed - okay, these things happen. But there was no need to make the feint in that situation.

I discussed the penalties against Brazil in detail with Ronald Spelbos. Ronald believes that you can coach players to take penalties. You simply need to take 10 penalties each day after the training session. I have my doubts. The decisive moment cannot be recreated on the practice pitch. The pressure, the tension and the circumstances will always be different in a real game. You could make a bet with Ronald de Boer and he would score 5 penalties in sequence against the best goalkeeper in the world on the practice pitch. And yet he missed against Brazil.

Codes for the video analyses

1. Line-up/formation
2. Defensive play
3. Buildup play
4. Attacking play
5. Defending against corners
6. Attacking corners
7. Defending against free-kicks
8. Attacking free-kicks
9. Attacking throw-in
10. Goals against
11. Goals for

By the way, Taffarel deserves to be complemented on how he used the information he had been given. He will certainly have known that Ronald de Boer always waits until the goalkeeper makes the first move. He then shoots into the opposite corner. So what did Taffarel do? At the very last movement he made an upper-body feint towards one corner, and then dived towards the other corner and saved the penalty. Taffarel beat De Boer with his own weapon by a hundredth of a second. Just study the videotape.

Video was a major new element in our analysis. Besides written information, we had to collect data for our video specialist Roberto Tolentino. These were then integrated into the video separately. This is why we watched games on television immediately after they had finished. Eurosport always showed the time on the screen, so we could specify exactly where the required images could be found. We also agreed on certain codes for the various elements of the game (see box). We assigned codes to match situations as an aid to Tolentino. In this way we provided the script for the videotape that backed up our written analysis.

I think that in the near future we will sit in the stands with a laptop, into which all kinds of data have already been programmed.

The large 'hole' in the right zone.

You will then need 2 people to carry out the analysis. Otherwise you may overlook important events that happen on the field while you are processing data.

A lot of work goes into such an analysis. This is not simply a matter of scope. You must avoid putting in too much detail, but you must not leave out any essentials. Why avoid being too detailed? A coach is always confronted with an overabundance of information, while he also has a lot of other things to focus on. He has to be selective. Just like a business manager, who cannot possibly know everything about his company, but needs the right information to be able to make the right decisions at that level.

I usually had no direct contact with Hiddink. Neeskens was the technical staff's contact. Hiddink only came into the picture if a separate explanation was needed. That did not happen very often. Apparently we did not leave many points open that needed further discussion.

The enjoyable moments certainly predominated in France. But of course there are always a few annoyances. The view from the reserved seats in the stadiums was not always satisfactory. Sometimes they were low down, and people continually stood up and blocked our line of vision. This only made our task more difficult.

On the soccer side, I was annoyed by the Dutch positional play during the game with Croatia. The defensive line was impossible. No one stayed on the flanks, so Jaap Stam and Frank de Boer frequently had to cover the whole width of the field. That cannot be allowed to happen. Asanovic was able to profit from this, because he was allowed to move into space behind Seedorf's back. That evening I felt that our analysis of Croatia had been in vain. But on the other hand things like that allow you to put your work into perspective. An analysis is simply an aid. On the pitch the players will always be confronted with new problems, to which they will have to find an immediate solution.

Restart plays

The most notable set play was the free-kick taken by Argentina against England. The players' reactions showed that Argentina had practiced this move intensively during their preparation. It was a

creative soccer move. It could have been a Dutch free-kick!! The English defenders were completely surprised by the pass to the player beside the wall and were caught on the wrong foot. It was a pleasure to watch. In the evening I sat in front of the video and made a very precise diagram of the play. That was one for my collection.

The battle for the coveted '98 World Cup was decided in France by two corner-kicks. During the tournament, 5 goals were scored directly and 15 indirectly from free-kicks. Penalties and corner-kicks resulted in 17 and 16 goals respectively. In total, therefore, 53 of the 171 goals came from restart plays. At 31%, this is a very high proportion. The Dutch team formed a notable exception, scoring only once from such a "dead ball" situation..

Corner-kicks

Sixteen goals came from corner-kicks. The photos on this and the previous page show how Zidane scored from such a kick during the final against Brazil.

A lot of goals were scored from corner-kicks during the '98 World Championship. Frans Hoek has examined corner-kicks and discusses the most important aspects:

Hoek: I have to admit that the experience I have gained in Spain during the last year has caused me to change my opinions about corner-kicks. I used to believe that it was only necessary to have a player guarding the near post. This gives you an extra player to mark an opponent. But in Spain I discovered that the role of the specialist is exceptionally important. If a corner is awarded against you in the Netherlands, there is usually no real danger. The ball is in the

The Dutch team often takes the 'safe' option of playing the corner-kick into a zone.

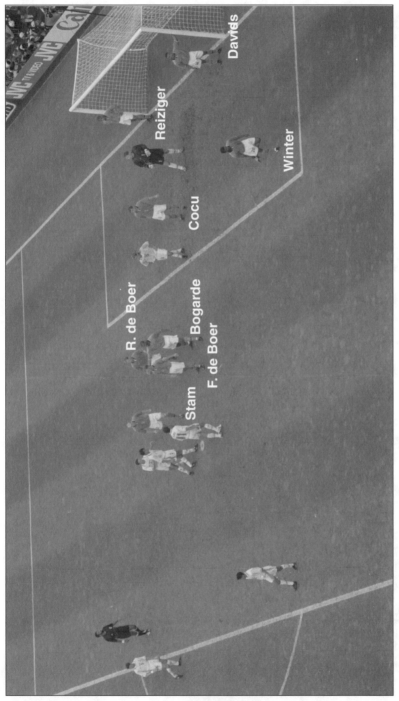

The Dutch team positions to defend the corner.

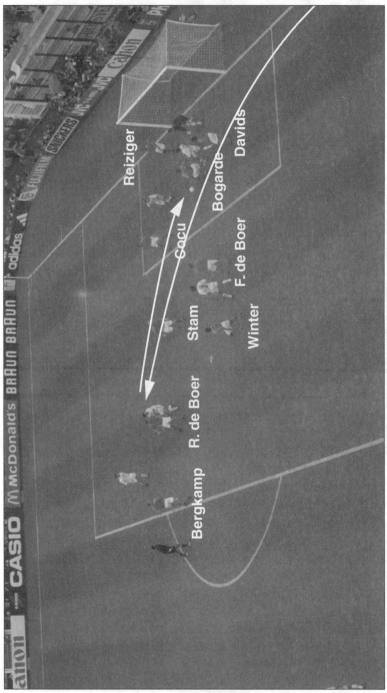

Ronald de Boer is beaten and Bogarde makes an error, allowing the goal by Mexico's Pelaez.

air for too long and the defenders have a very good chance of intercepting it. In Spain the corner-kicks are hit much harder. The ball often arrives head-high at great pace, with a lot of spin on it. The incoming attackers are also more dangerous, because they put everything they have into it. That is typical of the Spanish mentality. For this reason Barcelona now puts a man on each post when the team concedes a corner. Last season the man on the far post saved at least six certain goals.

There are a number of standard organizational aspects that you have to pay attention to. There must be a player guarding each post. These players can stand just inside the field of play. I regard them as the guardians of this area. The position of the player on the edge of the goal-area varies, depending on how the corner is taken. Then there has to be a second player in front of the near post. These are the four positions that always have to be occupied at Barcelona. We have also given some thought to positioning a man 10 yards from the corner-flag to distract the kicker.

We practice taking and defending against corner-kicks each week before the match. That is logical, because it can pay off in a big way.

The Dutch team is not good at taking corner-kicks. There is too little movement in front of goal, too many players stand still, and that is always to the advantage of the defenders. You have to make runs to create space, especially by running in towards the near post. This creates space at the far post, which other players can exploit. At club level you sometimes see players forming a screen to block defenders. Corner-kicks should be taken by specialists. Jonk is not a genuine specialist in my opinion. He just takes the safe option of kicking the ball into a certain zone. If you are going to play safe, you have no chance of scoring.

Twenty corner-kicks were awarded against the Netherlands at the '98 World Cup. One goal was conceded from them, against Mexico. Pelaez's goal was due to an error by Bogarde, but it was Ronald de Boer who was beaten to the ball in the air when Villa took the corner-kick on the right (see page 95 photo).

The Germans performed poorly in general, but their corner-kicks were extremely dangerous. The incoming strikers Klinsmann and Bierhoff, in particular, were always threatening. The success rate from these corners was very high. Bierhoff scored from Thon's right-footed, right-wing corner against Yugoslavia to equalize at 2-2 (see photos page 98). And from the left-wing corner just before, he headed the ball against the cross-bar.

Free-kicks

Twenty goals were scored directly and indirectly from free-kicks. The Dutch team conceded a goal against Yugoslavia (1-1) from a free-kick awarded on the flank.

Most free-kicks are hit hard at goal. Like those of Roberto Carlos, for example. On five occasions a goal was scored directly from a free-kick. Hiero succeeded against Nigeria, and Sierra against Cameroon, but the best directly taken free-kick was that of Beckham against Columbia (see photo 99).

In general there was not much variation in the free-kicks. One exception was the best free-kick of the whole World Cup, from which Argentina scored against England (see Figure 2, page 99). It deserves to be framed, and practiced during coaching sessions.

Penalty-kicks

In a deciding series of penalty-kicks, you know that you have a 50-50 chance. In such a situation you have to remain calm.

According to a sports psychologist, the tension when penalties are being taken is different to the tension during the match. During the

Overview of the Dutch team's matches															
	Ne-Be		Ne-SK		Ne-Me		Ne-Yu		Ne-Ar		Ne-Br		Ne-Cr		Totals Ne-Oppos.	
Corners	9	1	6	3	4	4	9	2	7	4	6	5	6	1	47	20
Offside	4	-	5	1	-	4	3	3	1	3	5	4	3	5	21	21
Shots	23	6	27	12	19	13	17	6	18	9	18	18	20	5	142	69
Shots at goal	7	2	17	4	7	5	13	3	9	5	6	10	8	3	67	32
Yellow cards	-	2	-	2	2	4	-	3	3	3	4	2	2	4	11	20
Red cards	1	-	-	-	-	1	-	-	1	1	-	-	-	-	2	2
Fouls	16	23	11	16	18	12	10	12	22	14	24	10	16	19	126	109

The dangerous corner kicks of the German team.

challenges on the pitch you are on auto-pilot. You don't think, 'What will happen if I shoot wide?' So you should not think that way when you have to take a penalty. But in practice this is not so easy.

Goalkeepers can now move before the ball is kicked. Remarkably, studies have shown that the goalkeeper chooses the wrong corner in 67 percent of all cases. The Canadian researchers Franks and Harvey analyzed all 138 penalty-kicks taken at World Cup tournaments between 1982 and 1994, and found that 78 percent were converted, 8 percent went over or wide of the goal or hit the post or bar, and 14 percent were saved. The researchers advised goalkeepers not to focus on the ball but to pay attention to the penalty-taker's 'foot signal' at the very last moment.

The German researcher Kuhn had already demonstrated that it is impossible for a goalkeeper to stop a penalty kick directed towards the corner of the goal at a speed of 60 miles per hour. The ball reaches the goal-line in 0.45 seconds, whereas the goalkeeper needs between 0.5 and 0.7 seconds to dive across to the corner.

When I was the goalkeeper at Volendam, I used to take the penalties. I took 10 to 15 penalty-kicks every day after the training session and found that the consistency of my kicking became optimal. However, it is only possible to practice technique, and not the taking of penalties under pressure.

In the '98 World Cup Semi-Final penalty 'Shoot-out' Brazilian 'keeper Taffarel waited for a long time when he faced Ronald de Boer, which was good, because if he had moved any sooner he would have had no chance. Ronald took a very short and very slow run-up. He was very close to the ball when he kicked it. As a goalkeeper, in such a situation you can 'read' where the ball will go. If a player takes a slow run-up, he must have the technique to kick the ball very hard, and Ronald does not. Cocu took a gradual run-up and Taffarel dived towards the corner at the moment when he kicked the ball. In Ronald's case, Taffarel dived after the ball had been kicked.

Van der Sar moved too soon in a few cases, and was therefore beyond the path of the ball before it reached him. Dunga, the Brazilian Captain, took his kick very quickly, and yet Van der Sar was already beyond the ball. This is why it is always an advantage for a goalkeeper to have information about how a player takes a penalty. Even then, there is always a lot of luck involved.

CHAPTER 11

Analysis of '98 World Cup Goalkeepers

Author: Frans Hoek, goalkeeping coach of FC Barcelona

A lot of opinions about the 1998 World Cup found their way into print. Personally, I always like to know what such an assessment is based on. Expectations often play too large a role. If you expect the Netherlands to win the World Cup, then you will be very disappointed when this does not happen. That plays a role in your assessment of the tournament. The color of the glasses you look through determines what you see. This article is also inevitably influenced by the way I looked at the games and by my background.

I have no desire to discuss each separate performance by a goalkeeper, as frequently happens in the media. The readers of this chapter want to know the reasons behind certain developments and actions, and whether lessons can be learned and put into practice.

I start with a theoretical consideration. First of all comes the question, "How should a goalkeeper at the absolute top level be assessed?" Then I discuss how you can assess a goalkeeper on the basis of his goalkeeping and creative skills. This is illustrated with examples from the World Cup games. Finally I deal with the most important conclusions that goalkeeper coaches can draw from this World Cup tournament.

Assessment at the top level

How can you assess a goalkeeper at the absolute top level of world soccer?

In other words, what did goalkeepers contribute to the final results of their matches and, ultimately, to the results of all of the matches?

This contribution can be positive. A goalkeeper's actions can help his team to win, draw or achieve a satisfactory result (during such a tournament a modest defeat may also enable a team to reach the next round). The contribution may also be negative. A goalkeeper's action can make life difficult for his team, or cause it to lose, draw or achieve only an inadequate result (if a team wins, but concedes too many goals in doing so, it may fail to reach the next round). A goalkeeper may also make no contribution, if he is presented with no opportunities for making a decisive intervention in a game.

How do you assess this? Arriving at an assessment is usually difficult and complicated. Superficially fantastic saves at critical moments may appear less admirable in the light of cold analysis. On the other hand, apparently simple saves may seem especially praiseworthy with the benefit of hindsight. Many spectators are unable to appreciate an unspectacular save properly. Usually they will put the blame on another player's supposed failure in these situations, with comments such as "Bad pass" or "poor shot."

How can you assess a goalkeeper on his creative qualities?
I will try to explain this with the help of practical examples.

A. Goalkeeping skills
A goalkeeper's first task is always to keep a clean sheet. He has to stop every ball that is directed towards his goal. And if he sees a

threat to his goal, he must try to avert it as quickly as possible.

Goalkeepers are assessed on what I call the "last" phase. This is the phase in which he stops the ball on the line, often in spectacular fashion, or in a 1 against 1 situation, or from a cross. Personally I assess a goalkeeper primarily on the basis of his insight into all situations that arise or can arise in "his" territory. By this I mean the part of the pitch behind his team's defensive line. Can he assess situations, see through them, and make good judgements? Can he read the play and thus decide how to deal with problems before they arise? A goalkeeper often reacts after a situation has arisen. I want to know whether he could have acted before it arose, or during its early stages.

A few practical examples

Jorge Campos

Opinions about the merits of the Mexican goalkeeper vary widely. Some regard him as one of the best goalkeepers in the world, while others condemn him as a clown. The truth is probably somewhere in the middle.

In Mexico's game against Germany, Campos intervened with a number of decisive actions that kept Mexico in the game for a long time. He did this, with the help of a little good fortune, by coming quickly off his line to intercept through balls 10 to 15 yards from his goal. If he had not acted so quickly, he would have found himself in a one against one situation and the chance of conceding a goal would then have been much greater. Subsequently Campos made a very poor showing when the Germans did score twice. In one case the ball came through the middle and he failed to act decisively. The other goal came from a header into the corner, which he should probably have reached.

Kacey Keller

The goalkeeper of the USA. During the World Cup tournament I spent a lot of time in the USA giving courses for coaches and camps for players and goalkeepers. During the courses in particular, Keller was frequently stated to be one of the best goalkeepers in the world. Some questioning revealed that this assessment was mainly due to his performance in one game, between Brazil and the USA, shortly before the World Cup finals. Keller had a lot of work to do in that match, and his fantastic saves ultimately enabled the USA to win.

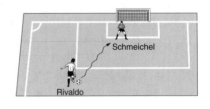

Things were different in France. Keller was in action a lot less, and he therefore had fewer opportunities to shine. Against Germany he only had 3 balls to deal with and he conceded 2 goals. One of these goals (see diagram above) started with a cross from the wing. Dooley missed the ball completely, which was a mistake. Klinsmann took the ball on his chest, looked towards Keller, and then side-footed the falling ball from close to his body, sending it into the far corner. Everyone said, "Fantastic goal, Dooley's mistake." My analysis, however, shows that Keller also made a mistake.

After Klinsmann took the ball on his chest, he looked to see where Keller was standing. Klinsmann then decided to place the ball in the far corner, and turned his body to allow him to do so. It should have been clear to Keller, from this movement, what Klinsmann intended to do. He should also have known that Klinsmann could not produce a powerful shot from the falling ball.

Keller failed to change his position and he only reacted after the shot had been made, by which time it was impossible for him to reach the ball. At the moment when he read Klinsmann's intentions, and just before or as the shot was made, he should have taken a step forward to his left to cover the corner of the goal. At the very least the goal would not have been so 'easy,' and he might even have been able to make a save.

Peter Schmeichel

Often said to be the best goalkeeper in the world. Big, strong, with a powerful presence. Very successful with his club team, Manchester United, and also with Denmark, especially during the European championships in Sweden in 1992. Nevertheless, he has to accept some blame for the goals he conceded in the decisive game against Brazil. In the 1 against 1 situation with Rivaldo (see diagram above), for instance, the shooting angle was very narrow and Schmeichel was perfectly positioned. Just before Rivaldo hit his shot, however, Schmeichel dropped too soon to the ground, creating a gap above his body through which the ball went past him. If he had stayed on his feet, it would have been much harder to score. And, of course, the long-distance shot from Rivaldo was not unstoppable. A good shot into the far corner, but if you look at the distance and the position of the Danish goalkeeper, you have to conclude that he reacted too late.

B. Creative skills

The team's intentions and its style of buildup play are important factors with regard to this part of a goalkeeper's task. The ball is too often hit hopefully upfield rather than with any particular intention. Coaching is important here, and all concerned must also be aware of each other's roles in specific situations. The goalkeeper's insight in relation to his ball skills is also a key factor. I can best illustrate this with reference to Edwin van der Sar. Many people praise his ball-playing skills, and I agree with them. Many people say that these skills are innate, and there I do not agree. In contrast to Chilavert and Campos, Van der Sar is not a 'natural' goalkeeper.

Van der Sar started as a goalkeeper who can play his part with the ball at his feet. Everything else has been achieved through hard work. First of all a goalkeeper must have a good overview, especially when the ball is played back to him. By this I mean that he must know where he can send the ball. We know that if the opposition play with 2 strikers, then there is at least a 5 against 2 situation in the defense. If there are 3 attackers there is a 5 against 3 situation, and if the opposition plays a pressing game, there may be just one unmarked teammate somewhere on the pitch. One of Edwin's strengths is that he almost always knows how to find the right, or the only, unmarked teammate, or is able to select a safe option.

Receiving, controlling and passing the ball are coachable skills. In this context, the goalkeeper's primary responsibility is his goal. If anything goes wrong, he must be able to recover immediately. A number of World Cup goalkeepers occasionally functioned as an 11th field player, but their fear of making a mistake often made them kick the ball upfield rather than choose a more creative pass.

In the Netherlands we sometimes bemoan the fact that goalkeepers do not have good ball-playing skills, but I regard De Goey as one of the best goalkeepers in England in this regard, even though he was often criticized when he played for Feyenoord in Rotterdam. This is because Van der Sar is the standard by which goalkeepers in the Netherlands are judged. But no goalkeeper can match Van der Sar's ball-playing skills. If I compare the general level of creative skills of Dutch goalkeepers with those of their Spanish equivalents, the Netherlands is far ahead.

What factors are important in a goalkeeper's buildup play?
Oversight and the ability to make the right decision come first. Then come the ball skills needed to put the ball where you want it. Finally you need the calm and confidence to play the ball in every situation. It is also essential that the whole team cooperates. Backpasses must be played as early as possible into the free space to the side of the goalkeeper, as far away from the opposing players as possible. The pass must be as easy as possible to control - at a comfortable speed, along the ground, and not directed at the goalkeeper's body. The other players must try to run into space so that the goalkeeper has as many simple options as possible for passing the ball.

This can only be achieved by practicing these specific situations as often as possible (see diagrams 3, 4, 5 and 6). Of course, a goalkeeper must have basic skill, but he must develop this. It is too easy to say that goalkeeping is only, or mainly, a matter of being born with natural talent. Dutch goalkeepers such as Fred Grim and Stanley Menzo are 'born' soccer players, but that is not the same as being a goalkeeper with good ball-playing skills.

A number of examples from the World Cup

Jorge Campos
A goalkeeper with good ball-playing skills. Comfortable with the ball at his feet. Only has an eye for the options close at hand.

Jose Luis Chilavert
A master of all goalkeeping skills. He can function well as an eleventh field player, but does not always choose the most efficient option. A genuine winner type. He has tremendous potential as a

Diagram 3

Diagram 4

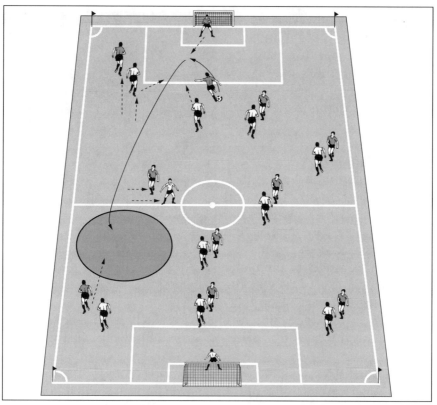

Diagram 5

Diagram 6

goalkeeper, but always gives me the impression that he finds it a pity that he has to share the pitch with ten other players. He is certainly not a 'team' player, but rather a genuine individualist within his team.

Claudio Taffarel
A goalkeeper with good ball-playing skills. He is not so good at deciding where, when and how he should pass the ball to a teammate. According to his colleaques, this aspect of the game is never practiced. This was the most successful World Cup tournament of his career, and he played a decisive role against the Netherlands during the penalty shootout. Not for the first time.

Fabian Barthez
The world champion, who also has considerable potential but is not yet master of his own territory. His soccer-playing skills are not bad, but he has problems in choosing the right option. A good goalkeeper, but he takes unnecessary risks by going for the ball when teammates are in a better position to deal with it.

Conclusions
Goalkeeping in general is changing and becoming more difficult. This was also demonstrated during the World Cup tournament. The goalkeeper is called on to defend his goal less and less. In addition, it is clear that a modern goalkeeper must have good ball-playing and creative skills, especially to enable him to handle backpasses. If a goalkeeper always reacts to a backpass with an anxious, hasty kick upfield, his team will probably lose possession. A goalkeeper must be aware of this and prepared for it. In addition, a clear 'job description' is needed to enable the performance of a goalkeeper to be assessed objectively. Top goalkeepers are increasingly expected to

be all-rounders with few weak points. Otherwise they will soon be found wanting.

I would like to finish with an example from the game between the Netherlands and Argentina. The Argentinian striker Lopez scored against Van der Sar in a 1 against 1 situation. According to the Dutch press, Van der Sar could not be blamed. Is this true? Everything was under control until Van der Sar took the initiative. Lopez waited and waited. There was nothing he could do. His speed decreased. His only option was to go round Van der Sar. But then Van der Sar lost patience. He moved, a gap appeared between his legs, and Lopez made use of this to score. Van der Sar was well positioned in front of goal and it was up to Lopez to take the initiative. Edwin should have waited. He sold himself too soon, and in a 1 against 1 situation that sort of mistake is immediately punished.

We saw a lot of goalkeepers in action during the World Cup. There were silly mistakes and blunders, but also tremendous saves and some impressive buildup play, in which Van der Sar is the absolute number one.

If we devote enough attention to good coaching we can develop good goalkeepers with all the necessary skills, using Edwin van der Sar as the model of a modern goalkeeper and modern goalkeeping methods.

PRACTICAL TIPS, PRIMARY CONSIDERATIONS, AND SUMMARY

The half-time break

Two key periods for a coach and the players are the half-time break and the first minutes in the dressing room after the match.

The main purpose of the break is to allow the players to rest and recuperate! Let them sit down and get over their exertions of the first half. Cups of tea are passed round and the trainer does his work. Look closely at possible injuries and observe the group carefully.

It is then time to address a few words to the group. Avoid generalizations and do not tell the players things they know already. If the team has played well, do not focus at length on the things that went wrong. Save them for the post-match discussion. Use the limited time in the break to explain why the team played so well. Tell the players what has to be done to maintain this level of play in the second half. If the team has a clear lead it may be necessary to stimulate the players mentally and to give them new objectives. You might say "We are starting at 0-0 again, and we want to win the second half as well."

If the team played badly in the first half, it is not necessary to point this out to the players again and again! The players know when they have played badly. Restrict yourself to pointing out what has gone wrong and explaining how to put things right in the second half. Above all, do not read the riot act too often, as this will soon have no effect.

Post-match discussion

Immediately after the game the players must again be given the chance to wind down in the dressing room and to come to terms with and express their emotions.

After this there should be a short post-match discussion, dealing mainly with mental aspects. If the team won easily, it may be necessary to bring the players down to earth by talking about the next opponent and the new objectives.

If the game was lost, the coach must never allow the blame for the defeat to be laid at the feet of one or more players. The team goes through the season together, and the whole team must take joint responsibility for winning or losing. The whole team wins, and the whole team loses. A goalkeeping mistake may have been preceded by other mistakes.

The detailed analysis of the match should take place at a later time. This could be, for example, before or after the next training session. The points singled out from the previous game can be used to give structure to this discussion. What was agreed? What happened differently, and why? How will the information gained during the game be incorporated into the drills during the following training sessions?

Playing with one man more or one man less

Every coach regularly has to deal with this situation. A player from his own team or a member of the opposing team is shown the red card and one of the teams has a numerical advantage. Many attempts have been made to explain why ten players can make life so difficult for eleven. If the red card was unjustified, or the underdog has to play on in the minority, mental attitude can play a huge role, especially if the score is still even.

Teams can experience problems when they have a man more than their opponents. This may be because the players are too dependent on the coach, and have not been encouraged to think for themselves about how to solve specific soccer problems. Some players can scarcely cope with the new situation - they desert their positions, and try to force a decision too quickly.

If tactical responses to these situations have been reached beforehand, they can certainly help when such a situation suddenly occurs during a match. Ideally the players will recognize the required solution because they have already been confronted with similar problems during training sessions.

A few tips that can be applied to 11 v 10 or 10 v 11 situations.
If an opposing player is shown the red card, it is important for the coach to analyze the situation first of all. Do not make the mistake of turning the team upside down. Some coaches tend to introduce

an extra striker immediately, but in nine cases out of ten this just plays into the opposition's hands, especially if the team starts to hit lots of long balls towards the strikers. Because there is an additional striker, the opposition's penalty area is more crowded and play becomes more cramped.

The extra-man situation must be exploited by high-speed passing moves. This forces the opposing players to do a lot of running, so that they gradually become more fatigued. When the team with eleven players has possession, it must make full use of the pitch, making the opposition play over as large an area as possible. If the eleven players can remain disciplined and keep their shape, playing from their assigned positions, goal-scoring chances will inevitably arise, especially if the two teams are fairly evenly matched. Discipline means, above all, that each player must stay in his position and carry out the basic tasks associated with that position as described by Louis van Gaal in the book 'The Coaching Philosophies of Louis van Gaal and the Ajax Coaches'. Coaches should devote a lot of time to this during training sessions, and especially during positional and small sided games.

What should you do if you suddenly find yourself outnumbered and the game is not yet decided?

The first principle is to keep the "one man more" situation of your opponents as far away from your own goal as possible. The second is to let as many of your own players as possible operate in their favorite positions. Make a minimum of changes! If you, as the coach, subscribe to these two principles, then it is a good tactic to ask your defenders and midfielders to play 1 against 1, and your strikers to move out towards the flanks. The opposing team's free man is then the central defender, but he will not dare to leave his zone because there will then be a large hole in the middle of the defense if his team loses possession (see diagram on page 114).

This solution keeps the number of changes to a minimum, and 90 percent of the players can continue to carry out their basic tasks. The possible scenarios associated with this solution are as follows:
- You play with three strikers and one of them is sent off. This is easy - the two remaining strikers move out to the flanks.

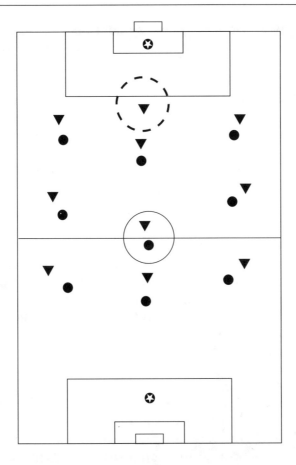

- You play with three strikers, and a midfielder or a defender is sent off. You first decide whether one of the strikers can take the position of the dismissed player. If so, there is no need to juggle the other positions. If not, substitute a midfielder or defender for an attacker, bringing the substitute on in the position of the ejected player.

- You play with two strikers and one of them is sent off. Can one of the midfielders play on the wing? If not, you can substitute another striker for a teammate who is not very good in 1 against 1 situations or is not playing well. Obviously the two strikers will move out to the wings. The other members of the team will play 1 against 1.

- You play with two strikers, and a midfielder or a defender is sent off. The strikers move out to the flanks and the others play 1 against 1.

Naturally the score, the difference in quality between the teams, and the ability of the members of the team to play 1 against 1 are also important factors that influence the decision to opt for this solution.

In any case, this solution is perhaps a good starting point for a discussion between the club's coaches.

The reserve player

A coach who does not communicate with his reserve players is inviting trouble. A player who is used to being in the team deserves some explanation when he is left out. You can explain your decision without entering into a long discussion with the player concerned. A short explanation of your reasons should usually suffice. The player does not have to agree with you. The important thing is for him to see that the decision is well considered and has been made in the interests of the team. This must be made clear.

Naturally, regular reserves within the squad do not need to have the reasons for this repeatedly explained. It is, however, advisable to devote attention to these players in other ways (extra training sessions, short discussions after a training session or a game). It is not possible for a coach to go through a season with his basic eleven. You need all of the players in your squad. Make time for everyone.

Try to let reserve players know what their role is within the squad. Imagine that you find it difficult to choose between two strikers. One is technically excellent, and good at playing one-twos. The other is physically stronger and therefore more dangerous. Ultimately you decide that the team as a whole will benefit more if the player with the better technique is selected. However, the other striker is a very valuable pinch hitter. You must have the man management skills to convince him that he still has an important function within the squad. Explain that his presence on the substitutes bench gives the team more confidence. His role can be decisive in securing a win.

Integrating young players

Statistics show that many young players give up the game when they have to make the transition to senior level. The causes are not just on the side of the clubs. Youngsters of 16 are now more likely to turn their backs on team sports in favor of an individual sport, which allows them to decide for themselves when, how, and how often they will practice. Material aspects also play a role. For example, a young player may prefer to take up a part-time job to earn some money rather than play soccer with his buddies.

It is therefore sensible to devote additional attention to young players who remain loyal to soccer. How can you, as a coach, handle this situation if you are convinced that your team must include sufficient experienced players? The integration of young players into the squad is therefore an important theme in the Dutch soccer world.

A lot of clubs already have a team that plays practice games during the week. This is a positive initiative. The young players can gain experience with the different technical, tactical and mental requirements that characterize soccer at the senior level.

But is it good idea to promote young players to the first team squad before they can hope to win a permanent place in the team? The best advice is to make the young players feel important by devoting special attention to them. You can do this in a variety of ways:

✳ Add an extra half-hour to training sessions just for the youth players. You can work both on their shortcomings and on teaching them how to exploit their strong points. These extra sessions can also boost the young players' morale, because they can see that the head coach takes them seriously. In such sessions, problems tend to come to light faster through the more personal contact.

✳ Give young players a few minutes of match experience if the match situation allows this.

✳ Young players want to be taken seriously. Talk to them as often as you can and listen to what they say.

✳ Show the young players, in word and deed, that you are not just concerned with the first team, but with the whole squad.

✳ Involve the experienced players in supporting new young players. They can ensure that the youngsters do not form a separate group before, during and after matches but are integrated into the squad as quickly as possible.

Not all older players are suitable for such a mentor role. Observe and select the players who are suitable. Talk with them about how they can carry out this task.

The most important tip: Take young players seriously, talk with them frequently, and devote sufficient attention to them.

Committee meeting

As a coach, you will often have to attend meetings of the club's management committee. Not to talk about team selection but to gain an insight into what is going on in the club and in the committee. You can also inform the committee members about your own policies. The exchange of information fosters understanding of each other's work and problems. It also enables you to detect signs of anything going wrong at an early stage.

Influence on team selection

Only the coach is responsible for picking the team. This does not mean that it is wrong to listen to other people's opinions - members of the management committee, players, people who are familiar with the club, sponsors, etc.

They can all provide you with valuable information, even with regard to technical matters. But all of them must be aware that you will decide for yourself what information is of importance for team selection.

A player should not be selected because the chairman or a sponsor demands it. On the other hand, there is nothing wrong in selecting a player when the chairman or a sponsor puts forward good arguments that help you to make your choice. There is a big difference between the two situations.

As a coach you have a duty to make up your own mind about who will be in the starting lineup. You can only do this if you avoid making all sorts of promises beforehand that you are obliged to keep. Never make promises such as, "I am not picking you today, but you will probably play next week."

A wise coach will never enter into detailed discussions with third parties about his team selection, and certainly not immediately after a match. And yet you have to deal with people who feel that they have to express their opinions about the lineup. Denying them this also causes problems. In such situations it is important just to listen. Do not discuss specific players but simply act as a sounding board. Extract any important items from the conversation and forget the rest. Always try to make time to listen. Having time for people is an important aspect of being a successful coach in the youth and college soccer world.

If you don't train, you don't play

Every coach should tell his players at the start of the season that anyone who does not turn up for training sessions will not be picked for the team. In professional soccer this is obviously the case, training is part of their work, and anyone who fails to turn up for training without a good reason can look for another team. End of story.

In the amateur soccer world, things are not so clear cut. Coaches usually have a smaller squad of players to choose from, and there are wide differences in skill within the squad. What do you do when, for example, your best striker moves to a nearby town, has a required class, or is on teaching practice and therefore cannot attend the regular training sessions?

If the team plays its games on Sundays, one possible option is to schedule the final training session for Friday evening. Of course, you will have to ponder whether this will not make matters worse, because other players will find Friday unsuitable. You will have to look into this, especially if the team plays in one of the lower levels.

A second option is to arrange additional training sessions for players who are studying or who cannot attend the regular sessions for some other reason. This requires the coach to work longer hours, usually without any financial reward. Nevertheless, such additional sessions are often the most effective solution. Such training sessions must then be made obligatory. Whoever fails to attend will not be picked for the team.

Clear communication with the players is essential in this context. State your reasons, and do not make any exceptions, even for your best player. If force of circumstances should make an exception necessary - for example, if a large number of players suffer injuries - discuss this first with the whole squad.

Substitutions

Preventing problems from occurring is one of the most important skills of a good coach. But if things are going wrong during a game we must ask ourselves if it is advisable to shake up the team. In fact, by doing so, you indicate that you do not have much faith in its style of play.

You do, however, have the option of bringing on one or more substitutes. When and how should you do this?
If you have a regular eleven, introducing a substitute should not be the first solution that you think of, although many coaches do think in this way. In some cases they may be right. If a player is not pulling his weight, or is deliberately ignoring the agreements reached before the game started, he may deserve to be replaced by a substitute within just ten minutes. Usually, however, a substitution should be a last resort. In most cases you have to ask whether you can do anything with the eleven players on the field to solve the soccer problem that the team faces. Perhaps one of the players could drop further back, or be given a new task. Sometimes it can make a world of difference if a certain player takes up a position ten yards further forward or back, or to the left or right.

The second option is to consider whether you can solve the problem by making positional changes within the team. If this does not work you can think about making a tactical change by introducing a new player. It is not always wise to act on a general feeling of dissatisfaction by making a lot of substitutions near the end of a game - for example, in a game that is being lost by a wide margin. You will have need of the same group of players one week later. Some players may suffer a loss of confidence if they are replaced during such a game. Players tend to feel that they are being made scapegoats.

The coach during the warm up

The usual practice is for the coach to circulate among his players during the warm-up, imparting final instructions. It is questionable whether this is worthwhile. After all, you have had the whole week to prepare your team for the match. If you feel the need to give instructions to your players at the last moment, then you have not done your work properly during the preceding week. Many players will not be able to take in what you are saying because they are so focused on the coming game. Moreover you may make players nervous by giving them last-minute tips.

The best thing you can do during the warm-up is to start quietly analyzing your opponents and your own team from the sideline.

Coach and referee

The coach can exploit the rules of the game to the limits of what is permissible. Ultimately, however, it is the referee who decides what is permissible. This results in tension between coaches and referees. This can have serious consequences if the two parties fail to respect each other's fields of responsibility. A coach has the key function of preparing his players for a match in such a way that they will give of their best without exceeding the limits of sporting behavior. The question is, where are these limits? The coach has every right to use all the means he can to ensure that the match ends in favor of his team, provided these means are within the rules of the game. Aggression can be injected into a match in a variety of ways. These can be:

- physical (tackles from behind);
- verbal (insulting remarks);
- non-verbal (behavior or gestures).

The coach should mention the referee during the pre-match preparations. Coaches and players are often familiar with the referee who has been appointed for the next game. His style and type of decisions have to be taken into account. This does not mean that the coach and players should regard the referee as an indirect opponent. It is always disappointing if a referee makes a wrong decision that disadvantages your team. Nevertheless, a coach should react in a mature fashion to events on the pitch.

This also applies to the referee. No good purpose is served when referees and coaches dispute each other's competence and skill. A coach has a right to push back the limits of the rules as far as he can.

He will always look for gaps in the rules that improve his team's chances of winning. It is therefore important for him to know how the referee interprets the rules. On the other hand, a referee must make clear where the limits lie, and how far coaches and players can go.

Good referees can size up the atmosphere and the situation without difficulty. They operate fairly in the spirit of the rules and are in control without being overbearing. A poor referee stands on his dignity. His attitude is, "I will show them who is in charge." This often arouses antagonism in players and coaches. Nevertheless, the referee is responsible for controlling the game and his word is always final. A good referee is unobtrusive and has no need to prove himself.

In a letter to all chairmen of amateur clubs, the Dutch Soccer Association stated that all persons on the coach's bench will also be shown a yellow or red card if they misbehave. A lot of aggression on the pitch has its origin on the bench, and many incidents are attributable to irresponsible behavior by coaches, their assistants and other non-playing personnel on the bench.

There will always be a field of tension between referees and coaches. This often finds expression in the form of provocation and aggression. Both sides must have sufficient decency, insight and respect to know where the limits lie. It would therefore be a good thing for more coaches to learn how difficult it is to referee a match. They should take the whistle themselves during practice games. Bert van Lingen has always found this the most difficult part of his job as assistant coach to the Dutch national team.

It is also important for a coach to intervene quickly to protect a player from himself. Have the courage to make an early substitution in such cases. Or at least call the player to the sideline and try to calm him down.

Criticism of referees is permissible, but should not be expressed publicly to the press immediately after a match. Keep your thoughts to yourself until you have an opportunity to talk calmly and rationally to the referee in private.

The rules of the game will always be used and misused. There will always be heated debates about decisions, and video replays cannot solve all of these problems satisfactorily. There will always be room for disagreement, but this should never be grounds for questioning each other's competence.

Fortunately there is currently a debate underway in the Netherlands about standards and values. Coaches at all levels should be aware that they need to set an example and demonstrate what is and is not acceptable.

Coaching Books from REEDSWAIN

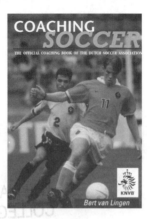

Coaching Books from REEDSWAIN

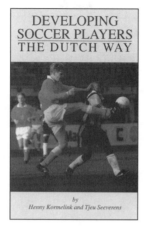
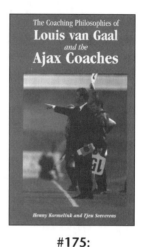

Notes

Notes

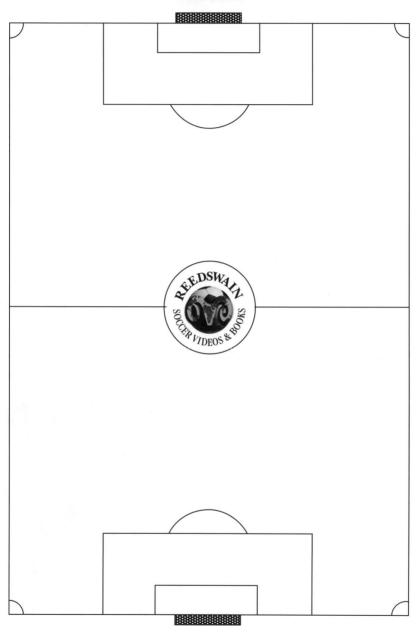

REEDSWAIN BOOKS and VIDEOS
1-800-331-5191 • www.reedswain.com

Notes

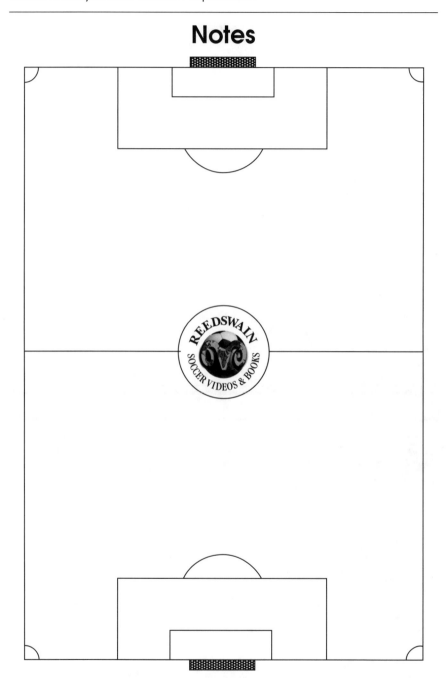

REEDSWAIN BOOKS and VIDEOS
1-800-331-5191 • www.reedswain.com

Notes

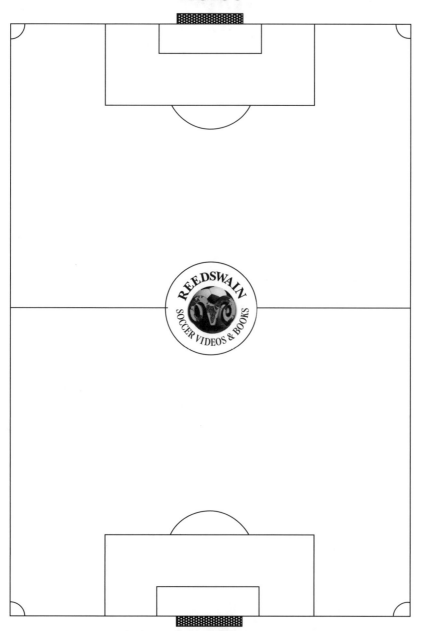

REEDSWAIN BOOKS and VIDEOS
1-800-331-5191 • www.reedswain.com

Notes

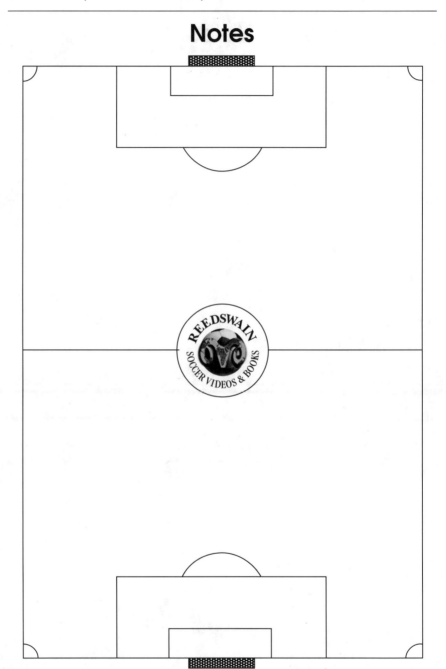

REEDSWAIN BOOKS and VIDEOS
1-800-331-5191 • www.reedswain.com